MEDITATIONSWERVE

Dear Richard:

You rock.

I see you

The guru is within.

Love,

larry@actioncompassion.com

MEDITATIONSWERVE

Your very own jackass sweetheart meditation companion.

Larry Li

ISBN: 1508612587
ISBN 13: 9781508612582

PERSONAL SUMMARY

My name is Larry Li. I spent my childhood being worried, anxious, and sick all the time. I barely slept growing up. I was always creating horrible scenarios in my head. I worried so much I made myself sick, and at age 20 I was officially diagnosed with Panic Disorder and Obsessive Compulsive Disorder. At age 21, the mental stress manifested into physical disease and I was diagnosed with Graves' Disease, an autoimmune condition in which the body attacks its own thyroid gland. I battled a general apathy toward the world, depression, and thoughts of suicide from age 20 to 24. At age 24 I was diagnosed with lung cancer—but thanks to a few miracles I am now completely healthy at age 28. For the past seven years I have practiced meditation daily. Without meditation, my life would surely not be the same. In fact, I might have ended it already. Without meditation, I would never have been able to see the gift that was my pain.

Through meditation, the darkness in one's own life can be illuminated. Through meditation, darkness, negativity, pain, and suffering can be transmuted into tools of transformation. Through meditation, we break through the illusion of light and dark and begin to flow with life as a grand process of unfolding and metamorphosis. Through meditation, we can find conditionless freedom within ourselves. The way out is in.

P.S.: I enjoy hip hop, punk rock, poutine, and stand-up comedy.

EDITOR'S NOTE:

The book you are about to read is probably unlike any you've read before. As an editor who deals primarily with non-fiction, it's rare that I get to work with material as quirkily unconventional as this, and I thoroughly enjoyed the process of helping to shape the form of the ideas that flowed through Larry and onto these pages. The book is written in a unique style, and my suggestion to you, reader, would be to focus primarily on the themes and feelings underneath the words rather than sharply on the words and forms themselves. The wisdom here transcends mechanics; read with an open mind and heart and I believe you will be grateful for the treasures you find when you drop into the place these words point you toward.

(One note about convention: Some wonderful quotes are sprinkled throughout the book; some are from famous people, some from non-famous people, and some from Larry himself. To avoid interfering with the book's flow, Larry has chosen to cite many of these references in an endnote section rather than directly in the text. So if you see a quote that resonates with you, you can flip to the back to see its source.)

Larry is a genuine and very individual individual, with great intelligence both concrete and indefinable, and it has been my pleasure to connect with him and help him share these gifts with you. Namaste (or Nerdmaste, or Weirdmaste… whatever your preference!), and enjoy!

Lynn Blaney Hess

TABLE OF CONTENTS

Let Your Roots Stretch into Hell.....1
I Am Your Pusher.....3
Mud can't hold onto water forever.....6
I don't.....8
At the center of duality.....10
"I wonder how much of what weighs me down is not mine to carry"[v].....12
A Worthwhile Practice.....15
A View into My Internal Landscape......16
Overwhelmed, Emotional, and Raw.....19
A Pillar of Meditation: Playfulness......21
In Response to Neil deGrasse Tyson… 23
A Poetic Passage to Assist in Mindful Breathing.....25
A Meditative Transmission.....27
A Casual and Ratchet Practice in Gratitude.....28
Gazing Raptly.....30
"Science is not only compatible with spirituality; it is a profound source of spirituality." ~ Carl Sagan.....33
A Guest Note on Freedom.....35
Mindful Breathing, Together.....36
Self-Love.....38
How Meditation Might Look in a State of Confusion and Self-Doubt.....40
Third Eye Ramblings.....42
To All My Friends.....45

The Resistance 46
Exhausting the Intellect. Featuring:
Third Eye Blind..48
Learn the Rules like a Pro so You Can Break Them
like an Artist..50
Seeds of Possibility Are Found in the Present. 52
Make Your Anger so Expensive That No One Can
Afford It and Your Happiness so Cheap
That Everyone Can Get It for Free 54
Meditation Is Your Sovereign Right 56
Resistance to Meditation..58
Airplane 60
Thunderclap Meditation 62
"We've Always Done It This Way" 64
A Second Visit to the Idea of Playfulness and
Meditation 66
Straight From My Heart 67
If I Didn't Meditate I Never Would Have Had
Dinner at McDonald's with a Schizophrenic
Man in Freiburg, Germany. 69
Meditation and the Practice of Gratitude 72
How Will You Hear It?..74
The Mountain 76
Sex and Meditation...78
Meditation in a Nasty Place 80
"Unwholesome action, hurting self, comes easily.
Wholesome action, healing self, takes effort."[xv] 83
500..85
A Meditation on a Multi-cultural Hamsa 87
Tattoo Meditation 89
Recollections on Generosity 92
"Yoga is like music: the rhythm of the body, the
melody of the mind, and the harmony of the soul
create the symphony of life."[xvi] 94

Everything Dances 96
Big Sean 97
Make Mind Civilized, Make Body Savage 99
Valentine's Day 100
A Meditation on Transformation 102
Carnivore 104
The Mechanics of Mantra 106
Tradition 110
Fuck off with This Whole Meditation Thing Right Now Please 112
The Esoteric Antenna 115
Let's Talk about Love Again 117
Disney's *Frozen* 120
Dr. Tang 122
Ego 123
If I Were a Nonsensical Lion We Would Have a Roaring Contest 125
Thief of Suffering 126
It All Comes… 128
Dū 130
Extreme Emotions 132
"Ever tried. Ever failed. No matter. Try again. Fail again. FAIL BETTER."[xxx] 134
You cannot force your mind to be calm 135
Look at All the Ways We Can Connect 137
Meditation Recollection, the First 50 Hours 138
Meditation Recollection, Hours 50–300 140
Meditation Recollection, Hours 300–500 142
Brave Men Don't Slay Dragons, They Ride Them ...144
Silence Is Better than Bullshit 146
Transparency Exercise 147
"All I can do is be me, whoever that is"[xxxii] 149
The Taste of Fear 151

"The Japanese say you have three faces. The first face, you show to the world. The second face, you show to your close friends, and your family. The third face, you never show anyone. It is the truest reflection of who you are."[xxxiii] 154
Today's Meditation: Just Say Hello! :) 156
Befuddled Meditation 158
"Man cannot remake himself without suffering, for he is both marble and sculptor"[xxxiv] 160
A Flash of Red 162
Selfish Meditation 164
"I have no special talent, I am only passionately curious"[xxxv] 166
I Should... 168
THANK YOU TO ALL MY FANS 170
Meditation and Creativity 172
Experimental Meditation 174
"My religion is not deceiving myself"[xxxvii] 176
Wild Minds Make Stable Hearts 178
Meditation on Public Transit 179
"I would rather be slapped by the truth than kissed with a lie."[xxxviii] 181
Meditation and Personal Transparency 183
"Just watch how our world is changing how people are changing. You contribute each time you show your mastery over your own choices for the essence of your Being rather than your reaction to the illusion."[xl] 186
"I myself am made entirely of flaws, stitched together with good intentions"[xli] 188
Obsessive Compulsive Disorder 190
Meditation and Enthusiasm 192
The Energy of Taiwan 196

A Poem by Daniel F. Mead 198
Cancer Check 200
Space Tiger 203
Turbulence 205
"Mastery requires endurance. Mastery, a word we don't use often, is not the equivalent of what we might consider its cognate—perfectionism—an inhuman aim motivated by a concern with how others view us. Mastery is also not the same as success—an event-based victory based on a peak point, a punctuated moment in time. Mastery is not merely a commitment to a goal, but to a curved-line, constant pursuit."[xliii] 207
Meditation Primer: Angry and Oppressive Environments 209
"I have decided to be happy, because it is good for my health"[xliv] 211
"Whatever comes, let it come, whatever stays, let it stay, whatever goes, let it go"[xlv] 212
Give Me the Whole Picture, Motherfucker 214
Running into Reality 216
Idealism and Gagging 217
Think Unconditionally 218
Tunnel 219
When Something Goes Wrong in Your Life, Just Yell PLOT TWIST and Move the Fuck On. 220
Forget Morality. Forget God. Forget Your Plans and Just Go. 221
Crybaby 223
A Visual Display of Meditation with Words 225
Here are some bonus meditation related passages I wrote after the manuscript was finished and edited. .. 229

INTRODUCTION

I am an incredibly flawed human being. I am prone to anger. I am prone to being overly emotional. I am reckless and thoughtless, easily pulled into the heat of the moment. I am fallible, inappropriately fastidious, and zealous from moment to moment. My mind is always whirling at the speed of a Tasmanian dervish and I have a serious hedonistic streak. However, even I can meditate, and there is *absolutely no reason you can't*.

Meditation isn't about imagining peace, stillness, or imaginary balls of light. Meditation is about familiarity and non-judgment. Meditation is about directing your conscious energy, which is almost always going outward, to go inward once in a while. Meditation is the idea that there is more to who we are than our fears and desires. Meditation is about exploring ourselves beyond what we like and we what we dislike.

There is no failure in meditation. It's okay to feel confused; in fact, confusion is sometimes necessary for an individual to learn meditation. It's okay to feel bored, tired, restless, angry, and crazy in meditation. Everything is okay. No one is FUBAR (which means fucked up beyond all repair and is #agoodcanadianfilm). All we are doing is taking the time to really hang out with ourselves. We peer into our consciousness with curiosity and consistency with the idea that all that is necessary for brilliant human transformation is simply the act of observing and witnessing ourselves and our experience of ourselves without judgment.

WHAT MAKES MEDITATION WORTHWHILE?

It is important for me to first say that meditation is much more about transformation than it is a stress reduction tool. Stress is a killer, and the ability to see through and reduce the stress in our lives is certainly valuable. However, with regard to meditation, the realm of relaxation is quite cheap compared to the treasures of transformation offered to all of us with a consistent practice. Relaxation can be bought, meditation cannot. A massage, a beer, a glass of wine, intimate sex, a hearty meal—these things can all relax us and bring us a sense of peace and wellbeing. Meditation however, although not separated from relaxation, also has the power to transform consciousness, the vessel which itself contains the idea of relaxation.

After eight years of consistent practice, when asked, "What makes meditation worthwhile?" I would say:

Put aside ideas of morality, enlightenment, and stillness for now. Let rest your ideals, goals, and aspirations for a moment. Put aside perceptions of meditation, of monk-ness and of goodness, of wisdom and insight.

What makes meditation worthwhile first and foremost is that it brings our mind and consciousness to a state of perpetual openness and freshness. Meditation gives us the ability to approach every detail of life with a sense of freshness, rawness, and beginner-ness. No matter how much more joyful, wise, or compassionate we become, we can begin each day with a sense that everything is brand new. No matter the knowledge we develop, the insights we illuminate in ourselves and others, no matter the techniques and tools we collect, none of them get in the way of the potentiality of the present moment. We can begin to really embrace and live the ideal that we don't really know shit—that the more we know, the more we know we don't know.

With meditation, the things that make you who you are do not get in the way of who are you becoming. The things that aid in your perception and analysis of life do not block your vision of the now. Your knowledge and conceptions of reality do not barricade you from experiencing the present. Your field of awareness is completely illuminated and open. Every tree, even the same one you saw yesterday, is new today. Every conversation, even the exact same message and sentence as last week's, brings a new communication of energy. Even the negative aspects of life begin to manifest with a sense of purpose and interconnectivity to the greater good.

With meditation, you find the insight and ability to be nothing. It is when you can be nothing that you can be everything. It is when the lake is still that the moon can be reflected. It is only when we are empty that we can truly receive.

HOW THIS BOOK WAS WRITTEN, AND THE COVER.

80% of this book was mostly written in after-meditation sessions ranging from thirty minutes to an hour long. 10% of this book was written while becoming a Taiwanese prune in the bathtub, effervescing among lots of bath salts and essential oils. The last 10% was written randomly, wherever inspiration struck, on my Steve Jobs phone. A lot of what I have written down feels like it was not from me personally. A lot of what I have written down feels like knowledge and wisdom from a place not fully my own. A lot of what I have written down feels like the down-trickling of illumination from higher emanations above, when I found the strength to be still, open, and even empty.

The cover for this book is a labour of love from my second meditation teacher, Chen Shi Zhong of Luo-Dong County, Yi-Lan city, Taiwan. He spent many years living in the mountains with a Tibetan Nepalese guru practicing meditation, yoga, Qi Gong, and martial arts. I modeled my creative practice with inspiration from my teacher, as he paints only after he has done a meditation practice. Furthermore, every brush stroke in his layered oil paintings is laced with his meditative intentions and mantras.

You may resonate with the idea that mind can influence matter here and may find it beneficial to gaze upon the book cover from time to time whenever you find the energy to look inward and shine mind onto itself.

IN A SENSE, MEDITATION ISN'T MIND OVER MATTER; IT'S MIND WITHIN MATTER AND MATTER WITHIN MIND INTEGRATING.

It is important that you challenge your own assumptions, beliefs, and ideas on an as-often-as-possible basis.

Approaching this book with a mindset of "Ultimately, I know that I don't really know shit" will benefit you greatly.

As the author of this book, I will fully and openly admit that, at the end of the day, I don't really know shit. After eight years of daily practice, I don't really know shit. After diving into the depths of my own mind and consciousness, seeing it transform and seeing my own life change, I can conclude firmly: I don't know shit.

Remain powerful and continually identify with the unknown. Notice the mind's weak but continual grasps for certainty and finality.

Rest in the unknown. Find comfort in impermanence and flux.

REMEMBER, THE MIND CAN RATIONALIZE ANYTHING!

Treat the positive and negative equally within to develop neutrality and transcendence. It isn't always easy to be neutral, open to possibilities, and non-judgmental in day-to-day situations. The place you can always practice first is in the mind. Practice always with the mind so that you can develop the ability to see things in the seed. A man once said this was the mark of genius.

As you read this book and you exchange attention with my essays and opinions, you will likely find yourself sometimes resonating with me heavily and other times being completely turned off. May I suggest that every time you are triggered by this book, whether it is positively or negatively, you take a moment to breathe deeply and recognize yourself as the awareness of positivity and negativity rather than the feeling itself. In this way, you can, if you wish, begin to identify with consciousness rather than mind. In this way, you can, if you wish, begin to change your relationship with your own mind. Every act of intentional change and awareness is like an evolutionary leap within your own being on the path toward inner freedom.

This book was written under the name "meditationswerve" because of my own abrasive and swervey nature. I desire to confuse and uplift you simultaneously while respecting my own rambunctious leanings. This is a book of *meraki*, a work that is linked to my soul, an essence that is neither purely good or purely bad—just pure potentiality.

SO HOW SHOULD I USE THIS BOOK?

First of all, you can use this book however you like. Duh. Here are some suggestions from me, just for fun:

You could use this book as a paperweight.
You may find entertainment in these pages.
You could hollow out the book and put condoms inside and go to the library with your lover(s).
You could hollow out the book and put illegal things inside and go buck wild with your homie(s).
You could use this book to see one human's authentic perspective on meditation.
You could use this book to motivate yourself to keep up with your own journey and practice.
You could use this book as a series of essays to trigger meditation and contemplation.
You could use this book as a zany companion on your own inward path.
You could use this book as a reference point on your own journey to self-mastery.
You could this book to try and see what is "meditation" in all situations.

You could read it fast.
You could read it slow.
You could read it fast then slow and over and over again to and fro.
You could read it now and then later and get something different out of a passage as your own practice progresses.

These are just some basic uses for my book that I could think of. I am quite confident you will find a way to create your own genius while reading this book. If I may make one final suggestion however: please, be your own master and continually evolve your own scales of life. Some have praised my words greatly and, although I am flattered, nothing is more important than your own inner compass and voice. No one can meditate for you. No one can save you and no one may. Know your will is connected to infinity and relentlessly seek that which is ineffable within you.

May your journey be true. May your life centers be aligned. May your words remain harmonious with your actions. Best wishes.

WONDER.

(I had the time to lounge around a while ago while I was visiting an old childhood friend. It was around 5pm and his fantasy football jam was about to start and I asked him if I could go meditate in his solarium as I was feeling a buzzing in my head and gut. For me, meditation has become a pleasurable necessity; sometimes it feels as if my existence yearns for meditation, to experience more than just my own mind. With daily practice, I can maintain a level of consciousness once unknown to me.)

Lily, the loving one-eyed dog, scoots close to sit nearby when I start meditating. I keep my eyes open for a little bit as I scan the room with my vision. At the same time I run my awareness with as much intensity and lack of expectation as possible with regard to my physical and mental state—simply noting every little detail of my existence at the time, opening up to the possibly risky idea that the extraordinary will take care of itself if we make genius of the ordinary.

What may sound like an agonizing mundane task begins to develop into a pleasurable type of work as mind begins to focus and sharpen while awareness expands toward infinity. I open up my mind to the ideals of self-opening, self-honesty, and non-judgment and slowly feel my eyes desiring to close. There is now a natural rhythm to my meditation. I feel I can work without trying after eight years of practice. My physical eyes close as what feels like an internal vision begins to open up rapidly. My mind and/or consciousness is trained to know that there are times when I want to be fully alert with my eyes closed.

The chatter of the football game in the background is becoming clearer yet more removed at the same time. It feels as though that particular channel of information is being totally absorbed into my meditation. I am not blocking it, I am not resisting it; I am able to completely integrate it in a way that it disappears into my consciousness. I know that sounds strange, but this is the only way I can honestly describe it. Through a practice of intentional choicelessness—losing the need to control—a transcendent form of control appears.

For the next hour I am completely awake and at the same time I am resting and rejuvenating. I find myself slouching a tiny bit here and there as more imposing and deep states of consciousness come and go. Breath feels ecstatic, light, and fluidly elaborate.

After I return to my friend's company, he starts to talk about how as you get older, things naturally get more stale. He feels strongly about his opinions and I can't disagree with many of his points. What I bring to the table, then, is the idea that meditation takes us closer and closer, step by step, to that possible place within all of us, that looks at the world with wonder. Every day can be fresh with meditation. What we own and what we know cannot get in our way if we have a consistent practice of seeking who we really are.

HOW LONG?

How long can you stay with a problem before you have had enough? Turning inward, how long can you sit with your anxiety, depression, or boredom before you need to cover or suppress it with something else? Does it make you curious at all to think what might happen if you were able to sit with that "negative" energy until it freely transforms into something else? How might your life change if you were able to truly flow with all that is inside and outside of you?

Once again I am nagging at you to think of the transformative aspects of meditation. Abandon perfection, relaxation, and peace. Seek truth and transformation within and all else falls into place.

Cultivate concentration of breath. Cultivate mindfulness of thought. Cultivate compassion toward the internal world which only you can access. Cultivate cultivate cultivate. Become the passionate creator of your own life, the life you have always dreamed to be. Be your own master, the captain of your fate, in whatever capacity possible, even if only in the mind for now. Be not tarried by fears and discomfort; know that this path of self-mastery is not easy but is most worthwhile.

Remember again that your will is connected to infinity if only you choose to allow it to be. Explore personal barriers, resistances, and conditionings. Your pain and your blockages are your own biggest teachers and clues. After all, "the obstacle itself is the path." Be you. Only you can do it. Be true. Only you can deem it.

Breathe in. Send conscious energy into that which can remain unconscious.

Breathe out. Send non-judgmental energy into a world that screams judgment.

Breathing in, you are aware of breath in. Breathing out, you are aware of breath out.

Begin to explore the genius in simplicity. Begin to see the power in a reduction of mind leading to a ferocity of consciousness that enables you to go past the personal barriers of self. Cultivate life from within and all things external begin to flow in harmony. As above, so below. Your inner world reflects your outer world. You see the world not as it is, but as you are.

A WORD ON TECHNIQUE.

This book does not have any strict teachings in terms of meditation technique. With humility, I contend that the word meditation is not so easily dealt with. If you are interested in technical teachings on meditation I encourage you to look for teachings around you and follow the one that resonates most deeply and authentically with your heart. Listen carefully to the guidings of the heart, which are often much quieter and harder to access than the churnings of the mind.

You will find essays in this book that speak of mantras and you will find essays inspired by Thich Naht Han's mindful breathing. These essays are meant to point your consciousness towards meditation, using words as a gentle reminder of the depth of what is within.

In my daily affairs, I teach meditation based on what I intuit to be most suitable for the seeker at the time. One person may benefit greatly from mantra meditation while another may benefit from a moving meditation. Some people can sit on the floor and some people, myself included, don't have the capacity for sitting meditation right from the start.

I would like to suggest that you read this book with an open mind. A large overarching intention of this book is to simply show you the magic that lies within you. I see no reason why you cannot find the magic of being within you if I can too. I must admit, if you were to look at my history and my behaviour as a whole, you would be shocked to find that I am one who teaches meditation.

"If you want to build a ship, don't drum up people to collect wood and don't assign them tasks and work, but rather teach them to long for the endless immensity of the sea."[i]

Borrowing inspiration from the above quote, I want to inspire you to meditate by showing you a glimpse of the freedom, magic, and transformation offered by this practice, of which only you can be the master. Many teachers and teachings are widely available; however, teachers can only guide you towards the truth within—the work must be done by you. If you are eager to meditate, simply start a sitting practice of five minutes a day, at the same time every day. Just sit down and let the mind express itself without your intervention. By simply directing conscious energy into the mundane you will begin to develop focus and non-judgment. From a solid foundation of consistent practice, you will find the next step on your path. Let your practice speak louder than the endless questions of the mind.

Note the preconceptions you have for meditation now and gently put them aside. I hope you enjoy this book.

This marks the end of the introductory section. The rest of the book is a collection of meditation related essays and passages chaotically organized so that hopefully you can open any random page and find something to resonate with. The swervey and disorganized nature of the book represents my personal mental chaos in relation to meditation. I want to say lastly that I am really no authority figure on meditation and consciousness. After 5000 hours of meditation practice I feel like I have barely just begun to understand the depths of consciousness. I wish you the very best on your own personal journey.

LET YOUR ROOTS STRETCH INTO HELL

When you are sad...you can still meditate.
When you are lost...you can still meditate.
When you are breaking, you are shattering into a new self.

The tiniest sparkle of clarity within. The tiniest glimmer of light ahead. Look at them with curiosity, and suddenly they dance for you. The dance of change. The fire of evolution. Sit within the storm and open to the idea that there is a center of clarity within all chaos.

Burning. Burning. Burning.
Deconstructing. Deconstructing. Deconstructing.

Oh, friends, may I be so frank as to say:
When you are sad...you are sad for yourself.
When you are lost...you are lost for yourself.
When you are suffocating, you are breathing into a new self.

The smallest whisper of courage within. The subtlest touch of love. Search high and low for the resistances within. Resistance to self-acceptance. Resistance to self-love. Fragmentation and civil wars of the mind. Smile upon them and allow your own confusion to lecture you. The message is always being transmitted.

Oh, friends, may I continue to nag you so:
When you are sad…you have to own your sadness.
When you are lost…you have to focus on your confusion.
When you are struggling, you are stretching into a new self; some will even tell you that you can stretch beyond self.

A piece of focus here. A piece of diligence there. Savour the good, study the bad. Collect, contemplate, and throw away. Throw away. Throw away. Throw away. This game of games is ultimately thrown away.

On and on and on, the meditation floats on. Through violent waves and sunny surfs, meditation is observance without a curse. Without praise and without condemning, the eye of balance continues expanding.

Disequilibrium coming into equilibrium. Desires coming into understanding. The fruits of meditation grow and grow without any pondering or planning.

Oh, my dear seekers, water the roots of your understanding and stretch them vigorously toward the abyss. For when you reach the depths of darkness with your toes, your hands will be bathed in light.

I AM YOUR PUSHER

You have to be a pusher to succeed in meditation. You'll have to make extra space in your mind for this discussion if you have not yet come to understand that there is no such thing as a bad meditation. A guitar string needs to be loose and tight at the same time to resonate. This piece leans to the principle of tightening. All aspects of humanity, including tenacity and aggression, have a place in meditation. The inward landscape is fraught with paradox, so embrace cognitive dissonance and let it push your boundaries of thinking, logic, and feeling. Going beyond your current limits is an awkward and magical journey, of which only you can be the master.

Push push push!

Push the comfort zone.

Push your own conscious trajectory in ways seemingly unhelpful or intimidating.

"Open at your own speed, but open.
Dig what's happening to you.
By 'dig' I mean get into it. There are lessons for you there. And when it gets uncomfortable, that's an important time to open and dig."[ii]

With every thought, every emotion, every intention, you push the limits of your understanding. Which aspects of my mental realm project me toward freedom? Which aspects ensnare me? Am I willing to break bonds for freedom, knowing pain is bound to programming? When you feel encumbered and can push no longer, you contemplate why it is you push. Everything that keeps you awake at night you contemplate. Meanwhile, you make love to the present while simultaneously studying and enjoying your projections for the future. I know, I am asking for a lot. Amidst it all, you are autonomous and empowered. The path of the pusher is intense but always reflected in allegiance to truth. To what is. You can't fail in meditation if you are being honest and mindful with yourself.

You do this all without judgment somehow. Somehow you find a way. Somehow you transform your consciousness into being able to exert massive energy without needing to latch onto any notions of results. Somehow, after you have given up trying and you have simply begun doing, mind completely revolutionizes.

Through this you become powerful in your mind, because you were willing to challenge all your own personal notions of power and righteousness day after day. You have no choice but to live in clarity. Alignment follows the whole of your being like a shadow.

"I don't like to be out of my comfort zone, which is about a half an inch wide."[iii]

Meditation will lead you to impossible comfort. But the whole task is to run into the discomfort within little by little, or, as you choose. Perhaps today is a day for a bold step. Perhaps this day is better for a confident but tiny step. Perhaps you are one audacious enough to tell me you are without discomfort within?

Do not confuse me and think I am advocating pain. To attempt further clarity, I contend there is almost always pain within, even in the most serene of settings. I've never met one who was not encumbered by demons and lifted by angels all at the same time.

To deny that you have dissatisfaction within you is poison. Feelings unfelt fester into mental tumours. I say this wide-eyed, smiling, baring teeth—do not underestimate the enslavement you can give yourself.

Give yourself the gift of meditation. Bring yourself to yourself again and again. Do it with a broad cerebellum and deep heart and go at it all without judgment. Start within.

Push. Push. Push.

"Bite, Chew, Suck"[iv]

MUD CAN'T HOLD ONTO WATER FOREVER

Meditation was difficult today. Even after eight years of practice, it is not always easy to engage my energy inward. My mind was filled with stress and questions while my ambition created anxiety about the future. I knew that meditation would be very fruitful and useful today but still I resisted. I tried to escape from myself anyway possible with every distraction I could think of but all methods of avoidance only got me halfway on the road of satisfaction and peace.

I finally took a meditative seat at 5:45pm. The first ten minutes were not exactly quiet. I moved around a lot and felt the negative energy stir and pound within my being. I made heavy sighing noises and felt unnatural in my own breathing. Despite the less than perfect internal circumstances, I remembered my ideals and trusted the process.

Attend to your negativity. Attend to your sensitivity. Attend to your anxiety. Attend to your stress and attend to your inner world. Just listen and hangout with all that is without judgment and create space for your negativity to move and transform I kept telling myself. Attend to yourself, even if you don't like yourself in this moment - just allow it all.

So I sat there for another thirty minutes. Choosing to be choice-less. I chose to go into that which I resisted and I just listened intently without expectation. With each passing moment, with each passing breathe, I felt my awareness expand and my perspective begin to transform. The stress wasn't necessarily gone, but it was transformed. That which was appropriate for my evolution maintained and all else began to fall away. Beams of bliss began to pierce through clouds of anxiety, negativity, and self made obstructions...

Many meditation teachers assert that our consciousness is like water. Even the muddiest of waters begin to clear when we learn to be still. The mud cannot stain you they say. The mud simply falls away when the conditions allow them to. Today, I have to deeply agree.

I DON'T

I don't meditate because I want to be saintly; I meditate so I can sin compassionately.

I don't meditate because I love silence; I meditate so I can hear more than noise.

I don't meditate because I want to be alone; I meditate so I can connect with clarity.

I don't meditate to run away from reality; I am trying to find the capacity of mind to dive into a new day head first, everyday.

I don't meditate to change myself. Yes. Tyler Durden says Self improvement is masturbation but I understand the paradoxical nature of our work here. Even if my ego is eyeing the prize, the work is just being here, now.

I don't meditate because I desire stillness; I desire stillness because I meditate.

I don't meditate to be better than others; I meditate to feel better in my own skin.

I don't meditate because I am a workaholic; I meditate because I see it as a necessary element to freedom.

I don't meditate because I am hardworking; I meditate because I am lazy.

I don't meditate because I am antisocial; I meditate to harmonize the space from which social constructs form.

I don't meditate because I am seeking enlightenment; I meditate because I am seeking self preservation of the highest order.

AT THE CENTER OF DUALITY

I am Yin. I am Yang.
I am Strong. I am Weak.
I am Male. I am Female.
I am Action. I am Inaction.
I am Positive. I am Negative.
I am a Sinner. I am a Saint.
I am a Smoker. I am a monk.
The darkest of evils with them I have bunked.

I am Shiva. I am Shakti.
I am Motion. I am Stillness.
I am Up. I am Down.
I am Chaos. I am Design.
I am Left. I am Right.
I am Right. I am Wrong.
I am Morality. I am Maliciousness.
The shifting of sands marks the essence of consciousness.

I am Shaman. I am Atheist.
I am Artist. I am Scientist.
I am Logic. I am Emotion.
I am Shield. I am Sword.
I am Left Brain. I am Right Brain.
I am Tension. I am Relaxation.

I am Restriction. I am Freedom.
Beyond dualism marks a new echelon of meditation.

I am Sense. I am Non-Sense.
I am Void. I am Form.
I am Intelligence. I am stupidity.
I am Beginning. I am End.
I am Vipassana. I am Samatha.
I am Light. I am Dark.
I am Life. I am Death.
I am Sickness. I am Vitality.
Thoughts and emotions are not our finality.

You are consciousness. The mind is your tool. Transcend the realm of judgement and enter the field of possibility. Release certainty and again be free to expand.

"I WONDER HOW MUCH OF WHAT WEIGHS ME DOWN IS NOT MINE TO CARRY"[v]

"Sometimes I can feel my bones straining under the weight of all the lives I'm not living."[vi]

Why meditate?

So you can really feel your own negativity!

By studying and sitting with the mind, we give ourselves a gift of time and presence which can turbocharge your ability to change and continually evolve.

Why meditate?

So you can see your own pain from all ways!

By breathing consciously and bringing attention to that which can be left to the subconscious, we give ourselves a gift of openness and malleability. Sitting often develops humility, tempering confidence into a sharp blade of self-empowerment. Avoiding the downfall of arrogance grants us more space to change and continually evolve.

Why meditate?

So you can fully understand your darkness but not be weighed down by it.

Separation from light and dark is an illusion. To give ourselves the gift of non-judgment and concentration allows us to see the chain of dependency of all things internally and externally. Your emotions and mind states need integration, not separation. Sitting often develops spaciousness within the mind, allowing us to see and use negativity in new ways. Internally alchemizing the weight of the very real darkness in this world grants us freedom. When we are free to let the world be as it is, we are able to change and continually evolve.

There are rare teachers, but no secret teachings.

There are no shortcuts; the best shortcut is no shortcut.

Consistency, self-honesty, and a willingness to challenge your own mind. Every day. That is the way to meditation, transformation, and freedom. Study the breath. Study the mind. Study the body. "The Zen mind is a beginner's mind" (common Zen adage). The rub is that we must work to become a student even when we have the hands of a master.

There is no magic formula for meditation. Teachers and technology can transmit aspects of meditation, but no one can reach into your consciousness and meditate for you. The only way out is in. The only true teacher is you. Who else but you can truly know what is going on inside?

Reclaim your authority but remain a student.

Own your power but maintain wisdom.

Open completely but question it all.

"Ever tried, ever failed, no matter. Try again. Fail again. Fail better."[vii]

A WORTHWHILE PRACTICE

Meditation, if it is to be useful, must not come from a place of deficit. At first, you may naturally find that all the mind does is judge itself. *This is not good enough. That is not good enough.*

Meditation, however, comes from a place of understanding, witnessing, and non-judgment. Meditation says, *everything is okay and is this way for a reason. Now let's fully embrace the situation and continue on with our practice.* Study the situation as it is, bringing the mind back again and again to the core of things when it begins to fantasize about how the situation should be.

Meditation requires gumption. A certain consistent and enduring drive to keep pushing the envelope. You must become curious about your own potential and the limits of it. As you practice and as you take the time to give attention and love to your inner landscape, excitement, curiosity, and natural gumption will follow. You will taste the sweet nectar of self-manifested evolution if you seek it. The practice is repeatedly ensuring that your ideals and goals do not strangle the present moment.

A VIEW INTO MY INTERNAL LANDSCAPE.

(At the time of this piece of writing, I had garnered a sizeable number of followers online and I was asked to describe my conscious experience of the creative process and the path toward "success.")

To put it bluntly, it feels like a battlefield. It's a strange thing for the human to experience any level of success. It's like you get to a certain point and the mind, the ego, the more insecure parts of consciousness start getting together and plotting. They get louder and more demanding: "We've found something that works! Now we must maximize, capitalize, streamline, and mass produce. We must grasp life by the balls and get as much as we can before we are gotten!"

Then there is this witness consciousness. It's always just aware, observing, and non-judgmental. It says, *Oh, that's interesting. You think that this is the path to peace, fulfillment, and joy? I see. Carry on then.* And the ego is so loud and expressive I can barely hear anything else. The practice, however, is just to keep trying, even when the ego is doing everything it can to build something that will last forever in a world that is simply impermanent. They say when you are still enough you can hear the difference between intuition and fear. The energetic substratum of my ego/mind was almost always rooted in fear. Unable to embrace the idea that the only certainty is uncertainty. The natural flux and entropy of life will continue with or without you. The ego builds and builds but the witness knows that to move forward with grace, life and the practice itself becomes a continual letting go. Letting go does not mean loving less. Letting go does not mean doing less. A meditator is not a pacifist, he is a raging storm centered by a mindful eye. When they say no attachment they do not mean no enjoyment, I can promise you that. Meditation is an open palm.

You can't carry the whole world. As your awareness expands you will find that you let go of things naturally due to their heavy nature. We're not interested in mere comfort. We want true freedom!

"Flow with the world instead," say the Taoists. Before meditation I demanded the world fit into me and my personal constructs of what should be. Now I look for places to dive deep into the world whenever and wherever possible. The crazy ones say it's always possible. Just breathe and imagine your awareness as the yin-yang symbol; as you grow, the positive principles of life expand in concert with the negative principles of life. The meditative master stands in the center of the yin-yang symbol (known to the Chinese as the Taiji). The meditative master surfs the ebb and flow of life. The master (YOU) does not clutch onto pleasure or deny pain; rather, you witness with great compassion and tenacity. Compassion is not sympathy or empathy. Compassion involves an aspect of wisdom—seeing pain and suffering clearly is the foundation for freedom and motivation. We are interested in an unconditional peace. We are interested in an unconditional love.

This is the internal landscape of a meditator who has overcome ADHD, OCD, anxiety, and depression over the last eight years. The ebb and flow of life continues. The friction of simply being existent in this simultaneously cruel and beautiful world gives fruit to who I am as a person. As I work to expand my awareness and increase my concentration, all under the meditative eye of non-judgment, I expand. I become more and more myself—and at the same time, something is developing beyond myself. My personality remains, but at the very least I can say this—I have a lot of space in here!

OVERWHELMED, EMOTIONAL, AND RAW

It is when we are completely overwhelmed, emotional, and lost that meditation can be most potent. After all, dear Rumi asks us to break our heart until it opens.

I am in a very raw state right now and would love it if you joined me in a simple mindfulness of breath meditation. Find a comfy seat, engage your core, and display as much physical symmetry as is comfortable.

Feel the breath. Feel deeply the ordinary and what is normally taken for granted. The master is now you. Only you can cultivate your internal landscape.

Breathing in. I am aware of breath in.

Breathing out. I am aware of breath out.

I open to the idea that genius is hidden within simplicity.

Breathing in. I seek to break down all resistance to the present.

Breathing out. I know that to feel is to heal.

Breathing in. Energy cannot be destroyed.

Breathing out. All is flowing and ever changing.

Breathing in. Emotions can be like tidal waves.

Breathing out. I allow them to crash and manifest as they are, opening the channels of transformation.

Breathing in. I am aware of breath in.
    Breathing out. I am aware of breath out.
    Breathing in. I am.
    Breathing out. I am.

As I observe the mind's demands for more, I return again and again to my heart and my breath.

Breathing in. I am.
    Breathing out. I am.

A PILLAR OF MEDITATION: PLAYFULNESS.

I have a good friend. His name is Doctor Bob. He's doing his residency right now at a top medical school in California and it sure sounds grueling! He prompted the topic of playfulness and meditation today—so thank you, Doctah Bob.

When I see and hear that word, playfulness, I instantly think of a pillar when it comes to meditation. Playfulness is, in my opinion, essential to maintaining and developing a useful meditation practice. Playfulness is a support beam we can continually lean on when things get too heavy in meditation. At the end of the day, meditation is supposed to empower us. We might be digging up the darkness within and bringing it to a point of non-judgmental awareness—but at the same time, don't try so hard. Be consistent in your practice but remember that the action of meditation is not something easily forced.

Meditation is an inward movement, different from almost everything we do to survive the modern world. Meditation is a path toward freedom and personal liberation and anything that takes us away from that can be approached with a little bit of playfulness. Our own negative ideas, conditionings, and emotions are not to be swept away or resisted. Rather, they can be greeted with playfulness and openness. We can give ourselves a little bit of space around our ideals. We can trust the process a bit more if we develop a yearning for playfulness. As we gain personal clarity, we might see that it is sometimes a sense of mischief and joy-seeking that brings us our greatest lessons. We need to see the edge to appreciate the center. We need a little child-like wonder to remind us to unfurrow our brow and soften the jaw in meditation. I take the time to stress such minor things because meditation is all about challenging our own assumptions and that can be downright uncomfortable.

Just today, I struggled for the first ten minutes to go into meditation—my mind sorta jabbered and I pictured myself quitting. With consistent meditation, we gain the energy to interject with a kind of meta-playfulness within the mind. I greeted the desire to quit with a sort of smarmy monkey wave and entertained my thoughts. Rather than be controlled by the mind, I entertained the mind. In doing so, the mind became expansive about neural relations and networking. Making conscious what can be left to the unconscious allows us to form new relationships with ourselves and perhaps even chart new territories of the mind previously unimaginable.

That's the thing about meditation. You can leave it all to the unconscious and go on about your life. Something in you must be yearning for more if you have taken the time to read this far. It's time to really start respecting all the machinations of ourselves. Hidden in your deepest emotion is your highest wisdom.

IN RESPONSE TO NEIL DEGRASSE TYSON...

"The problem, often not discovered until late in life, is that when you look for things in life like love, meaning, motivation, it implies they are sitting behind a tree or under a rock. The most successful people in life recognize, that in life they create their own love, they manufacture their own meaning, they generate their own motivation. For me, I am driven by two main philosophies, know more today about the world than I knew yesterday. And lessen the suffering of others. You'd be surprised how far that gets you."

The quote above is a very pragmatic and elegant response by Neil deGrasse Tyson during a Q&A session on the internet hub known as Reddit. It was a general question posed to Dr. Tyson, asking him for his thoughts on motivation and the meaning of life. Now, if I meditationswerved, how would I relate this response to meditation?

I was speaking with a good friend of mine yesterday. Clayton. A young lawyer asking me what meditation could do for him. He spoke of a desire for more control, clarity, and harmony in his life. I told him meditation was an honest but obstacle-ridden paradoxical path toward his goals. I told him that meditation was a sort of pleasurable work on our field of awareness. We practice non-judgmental awareness so that we have a chance to peep into the gap between thoughts, the space where mental phenomena manifest. It is there, in the seed of things, where we do our work as meditators.

I told him that I spent the first three hundred hours of my practice feeling confused. I told him that confusion was almost a necessary component of practice; knocking on the limits of the mind seems to reveal infinity.

To jump back to the quote, Dr. deGrasse Tyson talks brilliantly about generating motivation, creating love, and manufacturing meaning. Inevitably, I want to add my meditative opinion and I would say that meditation breaks down the barriers we have given to the idea of love. Meditation breaks down the limitations we set on love. Meditation tills the field where motivation manifests. Meditation moulds the internal landscape so motivation is never stifled. Meditation is the concentrative and compassionate witness that helps us find meaning at every moment through understanding and the openness of our internal processes; magic can be found in the mundane.

Meditation nurtures the foundational structure of the human life in both body and mind. Rather than changing the world, meditation clarifies and cleans the lenses of perception through which we peer out at the world. Through this, change is both paradoxical and inevitable. It is through these channels that meditation empowers us to experience life, love, and motivation in our own way.

A POETIC PASSAGE TO ASSIST IN MINDFUL BREATHING

A candle loses none of its light by sparking another.

Do not convince yourself that you can be smothered.

Anapanasati, the mindful breath of the moment.

Naturally illuminating the faculties of mind, your inner world a magnificent monument.

You cannot fail in meditation.

Don't believe everything you think.

You cannot lose in meditation.

Simply let the untruths drain from your mental sink.

Sit and choose choicelessness; practice flowing with what is.

Sit and once again be a beginner, placing less emphasis on what you think is.

Breathing in. You cannot fail.

Breathing out. Let the breath sail.

Mind is not enemy. Thoughts not your master. Dig at your own being, allow self to muster.

Turn the lights on within, warmly greet dissatisfaction.

Superficially unimpressive, internally magical action.

Sit with all that is, let consciousness bloom to fruition.

A MEDITATIVE TRANSMISSION

More than ever, the earth needs strong men who have learned gentleness and elegant women who have enabled ferocity.

A CASUAL AND RATCHET PRACTICE IN GRATITUDE

Forget all my fancy words and their illustrations. Forget the paradoxical Koans and other holy scriptures. Meditation can just be a simple exercise of gratitude. Five minutes three times a week, whenever you want. You might feel a sort of resistance when you go to do this sort of thing—but it's fun to transform that energy rather than deny it. So here we go.

Thank you, Dr. Gallant. If hadn't been lucky enough to find you, I would probably have a nasty thyroid goiter and I would still be itchy all the time. I hate being itchy.

Thank you Dr. Tang. You saved my life and then enriched it beyond imagination.

Thank you Andy, Ariel, and Hank. You guys were major support beams for me when I thought I was losing my mind.

"Fuck ya awesome ya I lost some, of my mind, and then I found peace that was real. It's awesome it's possible. Goddamn right. I've been honest the whole time." -Kanye West.

Sorry guys, the singing bird in my head got loud all of a sudden! This is a casual meditation! (This may seem strange but my intent is to be completely honest and transparent.

This is how my mind likes to behave even after eight years of training.)

Thank you Guru Chen, you taught me harmony. What a continual lesson it continues to be.

Thank you to all my teachers. Thank you seeds of life. Thank you IHN. Thank you Uvic. Thank you Mr. Parker. Thank you Grandma and Grandpa. You fucked me up in the best way possible.

Thank you universe. It's so good to see how today will express and unfold. Sometimes you have a weird and even twisted sense of humour, but it's interesting. I wanna stick around.

Thank you to all the trees and plants in my house, your company is invaluable.

Thank you money—we invented you and it's out of control, but I can use you to buy maple syrup, and that shit is the bomb.

Thank you to my body, you've carried me through a lot. Thank you cells for working so hard and getting rid of them tumours.

Thank you bathtub. Thank you life. Thank you breath. Thank you for this moment that lets be comfortably sit with the idea that:

"All life is deeply connected to all other life."

GAZING RAPTLY

Rumi speaks about four essentials for the seeker. Four essentials that assist in awakening the bliss within. Four essentials that enable us to hear the peace in all circumstances:

Eating lightly
Breathing deeply
Moving freely
Gazing raptly

This short essay will be most concerned with the idea of gazing raptly and how this "skill" can be developed through the non-judgmental expansive awareness that we can call meditation.

Now, I am no master when it comes to slowing down. Ask the mirror on the wall and it will tell you that Larry Li is the most rambunctious of them all. I am impulsive. I crave fast things. Loud things. Reckless things. Everything I like is addictive, fattening, and slightly impossible.

However. The more I practice meditation, the more I find the energy to look at the mundane with a meaningful eye. To look at something with rapture does not mean to foolishly pretend that this blade of grass in front of you deserves your attention. To look at something raptly must be a natural arising, unforced, and without expectation. The more I take time to hang out with my own consciousness without judgment, the more attentive I become to experiencing the moment—rapture begins to come unasked. Meditation has transformed my mind enough that I am able to see the genius in simplicity. I see that Gandhi was not without genius when he said that there is more to life than speeding up. Through meditation, through the practice of developing single-pointed focus and non-judgmental expansive awareness, the ability to gaze at all things raptly naturally begins to unfold.

There is no doubt in my mind that William Blake had developed the ability to look at the world with rapture as he wrote: "To see the world in a grain of sand and heaven in a wild flower, hold infinity in the palm of your hand and eternity in an hour." I can't help but see Mr. Blake as some sort of Zen practitioner as he continues: "If our lenses of perception were cleansed, we would see the world as it truly is, infinite." After all, meditation naturally invokes a cleaning and transforming of our personal lenses of perception. At first, we can only gaze at our inner process with our eyes closed, but as meditation develops the state we develop becomes accessible with eyes open.

Meditation allows our minds to shift gears. Meditation allows us to see the immaturity in a conscious vehicle that is always in high gear. Meditation allows us to pierce the veil with concentration and then fully understand the veil with awareness. To fully understand and embrace who we are at this present moment is to gain the pathway to go beyond who we are at this present moment.

To fully understand who we are, we need to develop the ability to gaze raptly at ALL things. To see the life force connection in things that are seemingly separate. To see grace in suffering. To see the light of desperation behind malice. To see our divine but difficult process with understanding while holding space for our ideals. Keep opening, keep trying, and never forget that this whole process is a journey of self-love and exploration.

"SCIENCE IS NOT ONLY COMPATIBLE WITH SPIRITUALITY; IT IS A PROFOUND SOURCE OF SPIRITUALITY." + CARL SAGAN

I used to be very dismissive toward ideas of anything that I could not see, test, and replicate with my physical senses or rational mind.

If it was difficult to quantify.

If it was intangible.

If it was asking for flexibility in thought, I had a hard time complying or participating.

This sort of immaturity and non-malleability in thought was the same sort of destructive channel that allowed me to convince myself that those suffering from mental illness were just weaklings.

Boy was it ironic when I suddenly overnight I developed severe OCD, depression, and anxiety.

Faith was earned, not given. I doubted and even ridiculed in my head many of the teachings I read about. Advice from my father was almost impossible to swallow. I felt almost everyone was saying one thing and doing another.

Thanks to the trials and sicknesses of my early twenties, I met some really amazing people. I connected with human beings who were attempting to live in alignment and harmony with the universe. I was still a stubborn know-it-all bastard, but I began to stretch my mind a bit here and there. I began to meditate daily at the age of 21.

Day by day I realized that life is inherently complex and in flux. Change is the only constant. Entropy. Impermanence. The ebb and flow of the universe. The low tides and high tides of our life experience at play with millions of other beings. I found scientific explanations and spiritual explanations were two sides of the same coin. I saw that the left brain and right brain working harmoniously despite seeming conflicts was a portal to more. I saw that we can train the mind to expand so that we can digest paradox. I started to understand that meditation was part of the puzzle of human potential. I saw that science was a profound source of spirituality and vice versa. I saw that meditation actually welcomed doubt and conflict. Meditation is only interested in running into reality; not running away in any sense.

Carl Sagan knew what the fuck was up.

A GUEST NOTE ON FREEDOM

"The important thing is allowing the whole world to wake up. Part of allowing the whole world to wake up is recognizing that the whole world is free—everybody is free to be as they are. Until the whole world is free to agree with you or disagree with you, until you have given the freedom to everyone to like you or not like you, to love you or hate you, to see things as you see them or to see things differently—until you have given the whole world its freedom—you'll never have your freedom."

Adyashanti

MINDFUL BREATHING, TOGETHER

Hope everyone is well today! I am writing to you from a three star hotel in Cologne, Germany! Would you like to join me for a short mindfulness of breath meditation?

Well, my friends, in a sense, you can't fail when it comes to mindfulness of breath meditation. It might not always feel comfortable or peaceful, but it is impossible to feel the breath without being in the present. The challenge then becomes accepting the present state of your consciousness as it is.

"Peace is the result of retraining your mind to process life as it is instead of how you think it should be." -Wayne Dyer

Breathing in, I bring my full consciousness to the breath.
Breathing out, I bring awareness to that which can be taken for granted.

Breathing in, I take note of all the noise around me.
Breathing out, I observe all of the noise inside of me.

Breathing in, I seek to witness without judgment.

Breathing out, I give myself the space to fail.

Breathing in, I recognize failure is only an idea.

Breathing out, I allow my mind to express itself as it is in this moment.

Breathing in, I adopt an attitude of openness and playfulness with regard to my mind.

Breathing out, I will continue this meditation until I have reached a comfortable limit.

Nerdmasté my friends. The awkward unity of humanity within me greets the same humanity within you. Don't buy into external opinion. Be your own master always.

SELF-LOVE

Self-love is not a free pass. Self-love is work. Self-love is the type of work that you might even call Karma Yoga. It is doing all of the work but offering the work up to the universe. In other words: You act without expectation. You plant seeds but do not let visions of the future slow your pace. You plant seeds but do not allow the mutations of good deeds to cloud your vision. You plant seeds of trees that you will never sit under.

You do all this not because you are a saint. You do all this not because you are a holy person. You do all this because you love yourself. You love yourself enough to understand what it is to pursue an actualized life. You love yourself enough to do the things that your mind does not feel like doing. You love yourself enough to trust that your actions in every moment are in alignment with your highest beliefs. You love yourself enough to do the things that other people won't so you can experience the things other people can't.

Self-love is honest. Your practice and religion becomes simply not deceiving yourself.

Self-love is patient. It holds the ideal but trusts the process.

Self-love is wise. It sees the desperation behind malice and ill will.

Self-love is determined. It commits to opening up and starting anew regardless of external circumstance.

Self-love is united. Intentions, thoughts, words, and actions are naturally brought into alignment.

Self-love is playful. It is happy to fall and tumble.

Self-love is tranquil. You want to pull other people into your peace.

Self-love is visionary. It sees the necessity of every roadblock and obstacle, internally and externally.

Self-love is animal. It wants to flow uninhibited by the ego.

Self-love is risky. It wants to spread to all those around you.

Self-love is dangerous. It will destroy all that is false within you.

Self-love is worthwhile.

Self-love is revolutionary.

Self-love is the first step in the journey of a thousand steps.

HOW MEDITATION MIGHT LOOK IN A STATE OF CONFUSION AND SELF-DOUBT

I want to motivate others, yet I feel no motivation in myself. So I sit down and listen to my lack of motivation.

I want to heal others, yet my personal healing journey is far from over. So I sit down and bear witness to my wounds.

I want to spread peace, yet my personal life is rife with turbulence. So I sit down and trust in the turbulent air of this journey.

I want to be free, yet my life seems full of restrictions and limitations. With an intention for clarity, I sit down and investigate these supposed restrictions.

I want to meditate, yet I do not feel sufficiently qualified to live in peace. I feel guilty for having what I have, yet I still yearn for the things I don't.

Sitting down, I embrace all the churnings and chuggings of my mind. I touch the prickles and I hug the thorns of my conscious inner landscape. Complete acceptance of myself marks the beginning of a complete transformation. Through practice and experience, I recognize the limitations of my thinking mind. I learn once again to let go of what I think meditation is. I let go of what I think this moment should be.

I let go of my current vision, not because I am without conviction, but because I want to connect with the present. It does not matter how brilliant my future plans are. Nor does it matter how clearly I analyze and synthesize the past. All the machinations of the mind pale in comparison to the possibilities in this present moment.

In that moment of merging with the present, I am free. Every day's journey to that place where I can acknowledge that letting go is the best course of action still surprises me. The path is unpredictable, as are the fruits of meditation. Again and again I breathe deeply as I begin to understand how the Zen masters spoke of resting in uncertainty. Again and again I steer my crack-addled mind to the present moment.

In the embrace of the unknown, I am free to heal. I am free to inspire. I am free to live.

I just had to get out of my own way.

THIRD EYE RAMBLINGS

I have always been incredibly interested in the third eye. It was not something I was always comfortable with. Seven years ago it was a mere idea that I met with a skeptical smarminess. Now, after personal investigation and experience, I contend that there exists within all of us a third eye. This eye rests in the unknown and unseen, centered in relation to two physical eyes of differentiation and analysis. The exact location of this energetic, esoteric, and ecstatic eye can be varied. People from many areas of the globe reference such a thing. Although the icon and idea of a third eye is spotlighted in the swift growth of yoga in the West, it is an idea beyond traditions and cultures.

In Taoism, the third eye is often referred to as the *Tien-Yen* or "sky eye." In yogic systems, the third eye is referred to as the *Ajna* or brow chakra, associated with intuition and extrasensory perception. Christian Gnostics also contend that there are major references to the third eye in the teachings of Christ, especially in the book of revelations. Christ Consciousness, seeing beyond duality, is the opening of the third eye, they say. Furthermore, we see the third eye heavily depicted in all forms of Buddhism. In Greek theosophy, the third eye is heavily related and perhaps dependent on the pineal gland. The French philosopher Descartes was also heavily interested in the pineal gland. Hah, fluoride anyone? *Swerve.*

I truly believe the third eye exists. If such a wonderful thing can be found within me, I see no reason why it cannot be discovered within you, by you, (and only you). I contend that the third eye is intricately connected, like a dew-dropped spiderweb, to the non-judgmental expansive and concentrative awareness we develop in meditation.

My first meditation teacher, an accomplished heart surgeon, told me that we are antennae as human beings. Cultivating the antenna, doing Sadhana, yoga, Qi Gong, meditation, honouring ourselves, honouring truth—these are the practices that refine and transform our antenna as energetic beings. The universe RESPONDS to your input. The trick is to learn how to become more involved with the universe at large without getting stuck on personal projections. As always, with meditation, it is best you find out for yourself; these words I scribe are just play.

It's funny. I always wanted grand mystical visions. I sought after them with reckless tenacity. I have tumbled plenty on this TRIP known as life. But despite my efforts, I never saw visions, cool lights, or mystical landscapes in meditation. I would sink into the gap between thoughts, but I found myself restfully awake in darkness. Void. Spaciousness and potentiality.

It was only when I lost interest in visions about two years ago that I started having them. When you give up control, you can have all the control you want. When you give up power, you gain the ability to do what you need, when you need to.

When you are nothing, you are EVERYTHING. Argh! This TRIP is just LOADED with PARADOX.

To my dear followers: Thanks for allowing me to take a break from writing. I needed to take time and meditate on my personal intentions, beliefs, and patterns for a while. I was stuck on some stagnant energies that needed to be dealt with before I wrote again. My work for the past few days has been becoming a beginner again. Remember Shunryu Suzuki? A Zen mind is a beginner's mind, he taught. Constantly tear away at what you think you know so that you can be reborn fully again and again. Day after day, as meditators, we won't settle for anything but the truth of the moment. Day after day we seek to fall in love with the world all over again. Day after day we attempt to find the insight to let go of what has long passed. We challenge ourselves to maintain an "open palm" stance in life; open, not grasping. To develop spaciousness is magical.

My challenge now that I've come out of the third-eye closet is how to reconcile this knowledge so that I do not alienate myself from humanity. Some say science and spirituality are deeply compatible. That the tangible and intangible aspects of the universe are deeply connected. Matter opposite antimatter, form versus space. I have found that many mystics and scientists are actually saying the same thing, just in a different way. There are even scientists who believe that the third eye allows humans to see into the quantum universe. Would you like to hear more about my personal opinion on the subject?

TO ALL MY FRIENDS

Playing with my mind, I clumsily understood meditation.

Going into my meditation, I learned to lose my mind.

Sitting in meditation, I heard the whispers within the silence.

Finding subtle senses within stillness, I heard the yearning of my soul.

Obliging to my own calling, I shattered my own heart.

Shattering my heart, I found light bursting forth. And abandoned personal love for something I can barely comprehend.

I have lost my mind. I have broken open my heart. There is nothing left but here and now with you, my friend. Just this cosmic dance of creation and destruction. There is no more analysis before giving and receiving. There is no more judgment before extending love and understanding. Here and now, we are free to be.

THE RESISTANCE

I feel comfortably burnt to a crisp!

The fires of change swirl vividly in the moments that have just passed in meditation...

A part of me resisted the sit but a self-developed, familiar arm of meditation yanked me toward practice. The rest of my being complied with a face-scrunched smile. I have become well aware that I never regret going into meditation. I am starting to realize my current ideas completely collapse in meditation and that the highest enjoyment is to simply get on with it. But I am clumsy.

Still, an aspect of me resists meditation. The voice of resistance has evolved beyond recognition in eight years, but indeed, seemingly unhelpful energy remains. What is it that resists change and the present moment? What is the voice that once in a while calls and says: "Meditation? Again? What could possibly be new??"

Who says such things within me? Is it the Ego? Is it the one scared of change? Is it the one insistent on plans? Is it the one looking for a final answer? Is it the one who always carries a notion of insecurity?

Perhaps. Perhaps. Perhaps.

Swerving and falling into the familiarity within is meditation. Finding once again the inward path that I have carved through confusion and corruption is the practice. Right here and now reveals the practice; everything else is imagination. Nothing is to be forced.

Every time I find my way through the meditative mire, I discover awe. I discover the potentiality of the moment. I discover the new and uncertain where the mind is certain. My breath naturally deepens as I bring myself closer and closer to the present, the place where possibilities exist.

Once again I find: “A Zen mind is a beginner’s mind.”

EXHAUSTING THE INTELLECT. FEATURING: THIRD EYE BLIND

I am writing this piece after doing thirty minutes of meditation with a song on repeat. I didn't do this on purpose—rather, my iTunes was set to repeat this song from a mantra practice the night before. I am already seated in my meditation stool now, and the song on repeat is *Semi-Charmed Life* by Third Eye Blind

In my experience, we learn to exhaust our rationale, intellect, and logic in meditation. My path was one of doubt and skepticism. I investigated meditation and I tried to figure out the puzzle. I was clever, so I tried to change the world. I was not wise; I had trouble changing myself. Accepting myself. Being myself.

I saw systems of meditation. I saw constructs and rules. I participated in discussion groups where humans played with words in an attempt to enter the sublime world of communication and energy behind them.

In meditation, we embrace frustration. We embrace the idea that our intellect alone might not bring us peace. We embrace the idea that our strength alone might not bring us peace. We embrace that the idea that our discipline today might not bring us peace. We see that just rationale is not enough. We see that just logic is not enough. We see that intuition alone is not enough.

Meditation is harmonizing all aspects of consciousness. In harmony and in familiarity, we can go beyond. We can go beyond ourselves. We can go beyond our self-made ideas. We gain insight into self-made limitations in the conscious, subconscious, and unconscious. MAGIC. TRANSFORMATION. To go beyond ourselves we MUST know ourselves. Deeply. Deeper. Day by day. Step by step. Breath by breath.

After seven years, it feels like I have only just begun.

LEARN THE RULES LIKE A PRO SO YOU CAN BREAK THEM LIKE AN ARTIST

"The rules you were given were the rules that worked for the person who created them. When you're mindful, rules, routines, and goals guide you; they don't govern you."[viii]

There are so many rules. Regulations. Traditions. Cultures. Teachers. Celebrities. Idols. Gurus. Beliefs. Systems. Constructs. All these things can either guide us toward freedom or tether us toward limitation. In meditation, we learn to discern which aspects of our consciousness are arising out of freedom and truth. We just gently notice and put one foot ahead of the other, trusting the natural harmony of life. We trust that metamorphosis occurs with deep awareness; we let go of stressing. We learn how to operate like an open palm, applying effort without grasping.

I recently started practicing Ashtanga Yoga, and today the teacher mentioned that in his tradition, when they trained, it was ninety-nine percent practice and one percent theory. For every one hundred minutes of practice, his teacher would indulge the students in one minute of dialogue and theory...

"Learn the rules like a pro, so you can break them like an artist."[ix]

You can talk about meditation until you're blue in the face. It is a particularly easy subject to just hold in the mind and never put into practice. Not only is meditation a slow-blooming and intangible fruit, it is easy to ignore. I say this not to damper you, but to remind you that you have to be your own master, ultimately, in meditation. There are tons of different teachers and traditions out there. Some make big promises, some whisper gently. If you recognize in some way that meditation is important to you, then just begin. Carve your own path while respecting the prints of those before you. Just start practicing. Even if you feel confused. Even if you feel disgruntled. Depressed. Anxious. Restless. Just pick a consistent spot and sit down there a few times a week to start. Notice when your mind tries to talk you out of it. To repeat myself, walk your own road, but keep a map. Solitude is powerful, but no being is an island. What the world needs now is YOU.

"Following all the rules leaves a completed checklist. Following your heart achieves a completed you."[x]

SEEDS OF POSSIBILITY ARE FOUND IN THE PRESENT.

Meditation is just this. Just now. Just here. Just me. Just what is.

Things get pretty fancy pants around here. We dissect. We analyze. We synthesize. We abstract. We focus. We concentrate. We try too hard.

Meditation is just what is. And the what is, is often painful. Meditation is the embrace of what is, even if it's painful.

It's not a forced embrace. It's not an embrace because we are so strong and so good and so right. It's an embrace because we love ourselves enough to walk the path toward becoming whole. To become whole the negative must be embraced.

The ideals of the moment become revealed, but the practice is the process. Meditation is just here. Meditation is just now. Meditation is familiarity with the present. What is. What is? Go deeper. Try harder. Try so hard you gasp for air so that you can find hints on how to let go. Only when your current understanding is exhausted can you begin to look beyond. When personal dissatisfaction is completely illuminated, the internal evolutionary process can begin.

Then you must let go. Everything you learn you eventually throw away. All that knowledge and insight you develop—do not grow encumbered by them. Anytime you are close to certainty, abandon it! Return to uncertainty and embrace the empty state of here and now. Live in uncertainty; live in potentiality. Live in the magic of the moment. Use what you have, start where you are, do what you can. The seeds of possibility can only be planted in the present.

Meditation is just this. Meditation is just now. Meditation is just here. Meditation is just you.

Life will twist you and spiral you upwards, but don't get twisted with it. Be authentic so you can breathe deep with ease. This journey is all about YOU.

MAKE YOUR ANGER SO EXPENSIVE THAT NO ONE CAN AFFORD IT AND YOUR HAPPINESS SO CHEAP THAT EVERYONE CAN GET IT FOR FREE

"Make your anger so expensive that no one can afford it and your happiness so cheap that everyone can get it for free"; "Got some niggas nevah call me unless they need somethin, but I pickup, like WASSUP! Watchu need cuzzin?" The first quote is from internet user "happyheartmsce" and the second is from performing artist J.Cole. ;) (Is it appropriate to put winking faces in books? Doesn't matter, self-publishing. Normal is just a setting on the dishwasher, honey...!)

I used to be very easily triggered. Looking back, it is obvious that I was looking to be triggered. Anger and destruction were commonly-used channels in my early 20s. To speak in yogic terms, you could say I had cultivated a mind and body that were primed for explosion. People said I was a loose cannon—and I took it as a compliment.

You buy into a belief system and you buy into a way of being. Before you know it, you've locked yourself into some sort of contract. This is now the paradigm and philosophy that works best for my acceptable level of contentment in life. I looked at life as this inorganic thing I could put into a formula and control. I titrated and rationed my pleasure like a feral being. Avoid discomfort. Avoid contemplation. Avoid silence. Go the path of least resistance. Make a beeline for gratification.

You will get what you are looking for. "What you seek is seeking you" says our Islamic mystic friend Rumi. Your inner world reflects your outer world. I can keep listing new age clichés or I can tell you that because I was looking for anger and reasons to be angry, I kept succeeding in my search. The universe supported me in my immature quest for rage.

Then one day I met a healer who taught me the idea of expanding my personal consciousness. Working with my consciousness in an empowering and purposeful way. Learning to work with this thing called attention and awareness. Learning to take nothing for granted. Learning to be too tight and then too loose. Playing with the extremes until we find that OMMMM. CENTER. Resonance. Equanimity. Harmonization.

The more I meditate the more expensive my anger becomes...I used to give it away for free. How foolish.

MEDITATION IS YOUR SOVEREIGN RIGHT

You could go through this life just fine and dandy without meditation. There is already so much on your plate. Why even bother with an idea such as meditation? Who needs it?

No one really needs it. The human condition, with all its awes and awfuls, is incredibly adaptive. Schizophrenics find ways to cope. Drug addicts function among us without suspicion. The homeless endure harsh winters. We can repress. We can deny. We can close off. It happens easily. Emotions can be buried in the subconscious and deep into our flesh (*I'll deal with you later…aka never.*)

Not to mention that we are so busy. Right? Who isn't busy? You gotta keep busy! You gotta move it - shake it - produce it. You gotta want it. You gotta work for it. "You gotta be bold, you gotta be bad, you gotta be wiser. You gotta be hard, you gotta be tough, you gotta be stronger."[xi] Move move move. Analyze this. Calculate that. Coordinate this. Integrate that. Multitask. Focus. Synthesize. Deconstruct. WOW. This world is sparkling, this world is fleeting, this world is suffocating. MOVE. Rest FAST, Work HARD.

A dear heart told me that she felt worthless if she did not keep busy. She wanted to spend time just finding ways to be peaceful inside her own skin but could not silence a voice. This creeping, persistent voice said she was not worth the time. This voice said she was not good enough for self-cultivation. This voice said that if she wasn't doing something for the world she was not worthwhile. This voice, partly manifesting from patriarchal Asian culture, said that to put herself as the number one priority was troubling. Oh dear soul, how the conditionings of the world have stained you. How the maliciousness of humanity, both intentional and unintentional, have stained your thought paradigms.

Come now, friend. Come now, stranger. Come now, all who wish to hear. You can never be stained. You can never be tarnished. You can always begin again. You can always create again. In your heart. In your mind. In your own garden of awareness, you can sprout seeds of change again and again. This is your sovereign right. You are worthwhile. You have wonders inside you. Keep trying to find the universe inside yourself.

RESISTANCE TO MEDITATION

It is when we resist meditation the most that we need it the most. When our minds are the most restless and chaotic, meditation can be surprisingly worthwhile. You may not feel better immediately; you may not feel good at all! The struggle to get to the mat is real, my friends. On a day like today, with the sun shining, my mind racing, and my body pumping, meditation is the last thing I truly want to do. At least on one level, this is all I can hear: *Go play. Go eat. Go work. Go do anything but go inward. Oh no, no please! Nah, Nah, let's keep shooting our energy into the world! There is so much to do, oh my, we can't stop, won't stop.*

My mouth is full of Nutella, coconut oil, and hemp hearts as I write this. Intense sensations of creamy sugary hazelnut flavor overwhelm my mouth while my mind darts around like a wild baboon. I am bamboozling myself. I take a deep breath as I lay down my spoon of sugary delight. Hmm, there is another gentle stirring inside; a ginger but radiant whisper. A voice that doesn't use words: *I have been seeking you.*

It's that meditation (familiarity) I have developed with myself. I know that when I finally find the strength to sit in stillness; true activity can begin. I know I will feel silly when I finally am able to extricate myself just slightly from my personal theatre. When I finally find the vigor to root myself in choicelessness, I can be truly free. I might look like I am just sitting here, but on the cellular level I am quite busy. On subtle levels of energy, I am processing, integrating, digesting. Metamorphosis.

I have made it to my Zen stool. What a struggle that was. I can feel my heart smiling, but my mind is quietly resistant. *Meditation. Bah humbug! Idealistic tomfoolery. Naive skylarking. Isn't seven years enough, by golly? Why do I need to sit here again and turn inward? Three thousand hours and you're still messing with this meditation thing? This is some shit. Turn down for what?*

Breathing in. I am aware of in-breath. Breathing out. I am aware of out-breath. Inhale. Exhale. Breathing in, I am breathing. Breathing out, I am breathing. Breathing in, I am. Breathing out, I am. I am. I am. I am.

AIRPLANE

I am reminiscing. It's five years ago. I am a little chubbier and a lot more ignorant. I am 22 years old and I am on a flight from Canada to Taiwan. Thirteen hours in a little seat with not much but me, myself, and I. Within a few moments I am tossing and twisting in my seat. I am tired but unable to sleep. I stayed up all night beforehand to tire myself, out but adrenaline and cortisol pump through my body. I am Larry's restless dissatisfaction. I am Larry's raging impatience. I suffer because the act of settling down into the present moment is unimaginable. I am my own worst enemy.

The flight takes on a slave and master dynamic. I am a slave to my unruly mind. I am a servant to the whims and whinings of my personality. I am a sucker for the aches and twists of my physical body. I eat the airline food to pass time. I read magazines to drown out the mind. I blast music in hopes of making the time tick away a little faster. I try to sleep but I just can't, and my allergies are really pissing me off. This is not my inaugural airplane anxiety fest. Time to hit the aerial potty where I will jump and bash around with hopes of creating peace through physical release. My god, I am the most pathetic and sad boi on this plane. This shouldn't be such a torturous experience, but this is my reality. I am uncomfortable and unruly inside my own skin. I am a victim of circumstance. I am not strong enough nor wise enough to settle into the peace that is on this plane. I suffer because of who I am.

Swerve! I am 27 years old again. In a few hours I will be back in my hometown of Yi-Lan. My flight was very enjoyable. Yes the seat was small, and yes I would have loved to just teleport to Asia. My mind is mischievous and exuberant as ever—but I feel no stress or discomfort in my seat. I feel perfectly comfortable in my situation. This is my choice. This is my life. "I am the master of my fate, I am the captain of my soul."[xii] I am on this plane because I chose to be; no matter the circumstance, there is an element of choice. I choose to root myself into this seat and open up to the idea that there is peace everywhere. Find your center within. Find your peace, and don't quit; everything else will fall into place.

Dancing stars, flashing lights. Looking in, I find light. Truth in stance, stillness in motion. Merge yourself with the ocean.

THUNDERCLAP MEDITATION

It's 11am. Rainy Sunday morning.

I turn on my computer and reach for the mouse, ready to enter the matrix of entertainment, the virtual dungeon of distraction.

I'm tempted to wake up with a cup of Irish coffee, and my mouth forms a smirk at the arising of such an idea...

As enjoyable as that would be, however, something is pulling me to my meditation room. Something inside me is not so easily entertained by the internet, vodka, or coffee. Something primal wants to have a sit. A chance to be more than this.

Just then, the sky breaks and thunder begins to clap down from above.

I am now in my meditation room, sitting on a small pine meditation stool. My knees press against the hardwood floor, my mind barely associates with the discomfort as it begins to turn toward subtler aspects of existence.

Breathing in, breathing out, my consciousness is changing. Breathing in, breathing out, the world around me begins to flow through me effortlessly. I experience all phenomena internally and externally, fully, without attachment or aversion. Ideas of good and bad begin to fade as faculties of analysis are completely disengaged. I am a dewdrop merging with the ocean. I am empty so the world and I are one.

Thunderclap! Thunderclap! A roaring burst of energy through the clouds.

I am breathing in thunder.
I am breathing in the electricity of change.

Oh, sweet thunderous applause from above, please cut through me on this day.

May the crackling thunder alert me to my own ignorance.

May the crackling thunder illuminate my own false perceptions.

May the crackling thunder bring me closer to today, to this moment, to the here and now.

May the crackling thunder destroy the personal visages that cloud my ability to love and learn in the present moment.

Breathing in, I am aware of breathe in. Breathing out, I am aware of breathe out. Breathing in, I am. Breathing out, I am. I am. I am. I am. Sitting underneath the tree of thunder I no longer find the need to label myself after I am. I am. I am. I am.

"WE'VE ALWAYS DONE IT THIS WAY"

The most dangerous phrase in any language is "We've always done it this way," says Grace Hopper, oldest serving officer in the US Navy. Growing up, I would lash out at my family for considering my Mom's side to be secondary. "This is just how things are," the voices would echo.

Speaking with fire, "This is just how things are" is a complete abomination to the potential of the present moment. This attitude is, in fact, a complete denial of our sovereign right as human beings. If you are not changing your mind, you are not using it. (To swerve slightly—as a meditator and truth seeker, I am not here to preach to you on how to live your life; rather, I seek to empower you so that you feel a sense of potentiality in all moments.)

I can't help but wince and weep internally when the hard-working lady at the bank tells me that many Taiwanese don't even think about the idea of being happy. She says that's just how things are there, that's how life is. I can't help but roar and yelp before my meditation, thinking about all the pain and suffering caused by such ways of thinking. Taiwanese kids are pushed into studying 12 hours a day because "that is just how things are done around here." Human beings born into the caste system of India are either hexed or blessed for life because "this is just how things are." Corporations in North America, human-made entities that have more rights than humans—well, "we've always done it this way." What a stunningly common copout.

On one hand, I want to say that we can be capable of more than a Marxist revolution. Perhaps we can train ourselves to prefer courage over comfort. From another perspective, maybe wanting to change the world is a fool's errand. Perhaps the only thing we can do is change ourselves.

To bring it all back to meditation: Meditation gives us the capacity to make peace with the questions that have no clear answers. Meditation can ensure that our vision and ideals are not clouded by fear. Meditation can allow us to plant seeds of love without worrying whether they will bloom at all. To repeat myself: Start where you are, do what you can, use what you have.

A SECOND VISIT TO THE IDEA OF PLAYFULNESS AND MEDITATION

I really think this whole idea of playfulness is worth repeating again and again. Finding ways to make your work play and your play work might sound a bit idealistic or impossible—but why not try? See the elements and skills that you are working with at all times of your existence and look for connections. Swerve. Duck. Parry. Thrust. Dive. Look for connections. Swim. Jump. Crawl. Sit. Walk. Look for connections. Leave no stone unturned. Yesterday's picture is yesterday's picture; look at the picture again today with the new you. Your physical internal world is constantly dancing and playing in destruction and creation. New cells are being created amongst the apoptosis (programmed cell death) of other cells. Neurotransmitters dance in your brain, flowing and weaving through myelin channels of communication. A complex orchestra of signaling and communication is at play even while you sleep. How you CHOOSE to play with consciousness is your sovereign birthright as a human being. How will you proceed on this day?

STRAIGHT FROM MY HEART

When my thyroid was in autoimmune distress (Graves' Disease), I experienced a lot of weird symptoms. The most rabid of them all was an internal itching that I could not scratch. I would be sitting there and I would feel what felt like little tiny itchy ant stings two centimeters within my skin, all over my body, all day long. The sensation drove me utterly insane for a few months. I habituated. I coped. But I struggled. At this point, I saw an amazing naturopath, Dr. Jamie Gallant, who practices medicine in the Lower Mainland in Vancouver, BC. Along with a bunch of therapies, Dr. Gallant inspired me to take the time to shift gears and slow down. A very amateurish meditation, if you will. After a month of treatments with Dr. Gallant, I remember driving back home with golden rays of sun shooting through the pine trees. A warm gentle radiance. I suddenly decided to just stop fighting my disease. I just said okay, fine, I have a disease. From that point I started a dance of playfulness with my disease. I am no longer ill today

Playfulness is absolutely a pillar of meditation for me. Looking for the humor in every situation may seem unnatural sometimes. Looking for the grace behind suffering can never be forced. Although we want to move on and be playful, meditation is about immersing in the present, without condition.

When we completely take responsibility for where we are, we can begin to hint at recess. When we own up to the situation completely as an individual, we can find ways to smirk amongst sorrow. When we allow ourselves to be exactly who we are, without struggle, while looking forward, joy seeps through every crack of existence. When we are completely honest and aligned, internally, externally, physically, emotionally, and mindfully, we can truly be free. Free from our own machinations and free from the world's. Utter potentiality and spaciousness. First, we find peace in meditation; we choose to be choiceless. Then we take that peace we've developed in our own time and throw it at the world. Try finding peace in the world, in all situations.

IF I DIDN'T MEDITATE I NEVER WOULD HAVE HAD DINNER AT MCDONALD'S WITH A SCHIZOPHRENIC MAN IN FREIBURG, GERMANY.

I was fifteen days into my solo backpacking trip in Germany, and I had arrived in a gorgeous little town known as Freiburg. The area I was in was on the exchange between a sprawling urban center and a University town. The area close to the University was also where my hostel was (The Black Forest Hostel—make sure you visit if you are in Freiburg). Gorgeous mountains and scenery blended into the city; cobblestone roads and colourful umbrellas lined the streets where a stream runs through. I remember beautiful rays of sunshine dancing on the cobblestone as toddlers played in the stream of water that flowed gently throughout this section of the city.

I had spent the day exploring and walking and was finding myself tired and bored by about 7pm. I had meditated in random spots around the city all day. It was so hot that you couldn't eat without sweating, though. Near the day's end I found myself complaining I was bored, so I took a walk into the city. I was planning to go eat out of hunger. I ended up at a McDonald's near what felt like the city center. If I had never gotten into meditation, knowing who I was before, I would have never even noticed the man sitting next to me. Bald, pale complexion, soft blue eyes, and slightly skinny. He wore denim and grey-coloured clothes. He looked distressed and hungry. The gaze in his eyes made it seem like he was deep in his own world. Somehow we got to talking and he explained to me that he was on a mini-vacation, that he had two days free where he could be unsupervised. He was usually under the care of others as he was a paranoid schizophrenic. Now, this hit very close to home for me, as part of my OCD obsessional pattern was that I was constantly worried about losing my mind in one way or another.

I don't know why I had that irrational fear, but I did. The man told me about his struggle and his day-to-day experience. It sounded very tough. It sounded very difficult. You could tell this man did not have an easy path. He did not want any help from me. I felt great empathy for him but there was little I could do. I just sat with him awhile and offered to buy him some food. I walked back to the hostel feeling like an asshole for thinking I was bored. It's awkward how the plight of others can fuel you to live the life you know you can potentially live.

That night, I saw the same man in my hostel. In my shared room of twelve beds. He was four beds down from me. We met eyes respectfully but he kept to himself and I continued to watch old Seinfeld episodes on my laptop. I wanted to help him, but I didn't know how. I ended up writing a little one-page letter about some potential therapies that I had seen work with regard to schizophrenia. I wrote down some things for him to check out so that perhaps he could find a healing modality suitable for him. I believe everything is curable due to my own experiences with disease, so I was hoping to impart that feeling to him. I put the note on the nightstand we all had next to our little hostel beds. Minutes later I watched him quickly glance at the note, scrunch it up, and toss it in the trash. I am smirking as I write this, because in a sense I feel foolish—in a way, I was intervening in business that was not necessarily mine. Even though he and I had lots in common in an immediate sense, I should not have assumed so eagerly that he needed or wanted my help…you can't help everyone. You can only love them. Give them space to flourish. Every step on the path counts for something, and it isn't always your business to know more than that.

MEDITATION AND THE PRACTICE OF GRATITUDE

The idea of practicing gratitude had always seemed a bit preposterous to me. I remember reading articles that talked about how people who were grateful were the happiest. But how do you practice something you're not feeling, that's not "real"? Practice being grateful? I'll be grateful when I feel like being grateful, I thought.

So, basically never.

Watching my past self through personal memory tapes, I see that I generally only felt this thing called gratitude when I got exactly what I wanted. Prodding myself with honesty, I admit I rarely experienced true gratitude. It was a drama of egoic satisfaction and personal appeasement. Looking back, I see an endless cycle of extreme desire that always led to apathy once I got what I wanted. What I once salivated for would quickly become trash. The grass was always greener elsewhere, never here, never now. I was never in the present. I never felt connected to the here. I never felt at peace with the now. For reasons of nature and nurture, my eyes were always on what was lacking. My concentration was on what I did not have. I searched for dissatisfaction and I always found what I wanted to find.

Thankfully, I got sick as hell. Mentally and physically. My life was blown wide open, primed for transformation. TURN UP! I began to practice meditation with a sort of dastardly diligence. I didn't really want to, but I knew it was the bitter medicine my soul craved. When the ego cries, the spirit smiles.

As I began to walk down the path of meditation, I began to notice that this thing called gratitude would sort of percolate naturally into my life. As my internal landscape developed, so did the natural manifestation of positive emotions. The more I meditated, the more I experienced true gratitude. The more I meditated, the more I fell in love with my life. By taking the idea of not deceiving myself to its apex; I slowly and subtly broke down conditionings and patterns that did not serve me. Complete awareness is transcendent.

In meditation we are cultivating and tilling our own personal fields of awareness. Fertile and spacious internal landscapes naturally change our lives for the better. No one can till and cultivate your field of awareness for you; this sacred work can only be done by you.

HOW WILL YOU HEAR IT?

Don't convince yourself that you are fucked beyond repair. As the Buddha said, "The mind that perceives the limitation is the limitation."

Don't convince yourself that you can't meditate. There is no such thing as a bad meditation.

Don't convince yourself to be this or that based on transient externalities. In the words of Tyler Durden in Fight Club, "Sticking feathers up your butt does not make you a chicken."

Meditation simply makes you more *you*; whatever YOU are deep within will shine through as you make acquaintance with less-explored aspects of consciousness.

Forget opinion; just listen to the sound within. You may hear screeching anxiety. You may hear siren songs from the deep sea of consciousness. You may hear nothing at all and become overwhelmed by the deafening silence, only to be startled by the blaring honks of the "real world."

It matters not what you hear, only how you hear it.

I give a fuck. I give lots of fucks, actually. I am a whore for feelings.

Meditation is not about making yourself feel less in the name of some imagined peace. Meditation is about exploring your own capacity to experience more without adding on internal dissonance and external limitation.

To be unattached does not necessarily mean to be uninvolved. What we are trying to detach from are our notions of reality that prevent us from flowing with life. We witness ourselves without judgment so we can learn from our thoughts, accessing information beyond simply what pains and pleasures us. We might begin to gain energy from our thoughts. We might develop new relationships with our thoughts. We might find that consciousness has the capacity for radical transformation, all because we gave a fuck enough to explore life without judgment.

THE MOUNTAIN

I must be crazy. The mountain is speaking to me.

I'm back at Mt. Tolmie, the place where I really began to explore the frontiers and limitations of the mind. It certainly doesn't feel like imagination; I can feel currents of earth shooting into me as I stand barefoot on this modest mountain.

As I sit in the many meditative grooves on the mountain, I begin to recollect the past. Broken glass, cigarette butts, cannabis roaches, and used condoms hide amongst the blades of golden grass. I have broken a heart here and I have fallen in love here. It is here I learned to see all things as they truly are, impermanent but so profoundly interconnected. Are we not all on the same journey, near and far, for clarity and contentment?

I swear the mountain remembers. The mountain remembers how I used to be a slave to my own thoughts and emotions—dragged by the nose. The mountain knows that embracing confusion and pain is the first step on the path toward greater freedom. If you would grant yourself the gift of meditation, if you would play with your own programming and conditioning, if you would explore the limits of your perception, you might begin to see things as the mountains do: infinite, interconnected, and always in motion.

These words are not mine. I am simply quiet and crazy enough to hear the echoes of the earth. The earth and sky do not judge you; they simply witness.

SEX AND MEDITATION

The parallel between sex and meditation is an interesting one. To oversimplify, meditation is the experience of losing ourselves in the moment. Similarly, I now understand good sex to be the natural loss of our personal identity through union.

I used to have terrible performance anxiety when it came to sex. Before my shirt even came off my mind would be racing with objectives. *I want to make her cum. I want to be the best lover. I want to ravage and take her in "best" way possible. If there is no big orgasm, then sex is a failure.* My own mind would rob myself of the experience. My consciousness would always be ten seconds ahead of the present moment, unable to fully experience the magic of the moment. There were times I had difficulty getting an erection because I was so consumed with my own thoughts. Sex was a mission. Until she came, I could not enjoy myself. I found ways to combat my own narcissism. I love eating pussy and tossing salads, so that oral tradition in itself became sort of a way for me to meditate on my anxiety until it went away. However, I was not free. Not free at all. What the flying fuck kind of life is this?

With meditation—passionate non-judgmental observance of my anxiety—a transformation began to take place over the years. The more clarity I gained with regard to my anxiety, the less control it had over me. Meditation has given me a new kind of sex.

Meditation makes me empty. When I am nothing, I can be everything. My inner dialogue is quieter, or sometimes non-existent. My personal objectives and missions are just fluid notions that harmonize with the current moment. I am actually alive! I am in this world! I am naked and I am here with you. I can listen to your needs and feel the vibrations of your being. I can hear the callings of your body and I can peer into the glimmer in your eyes. I can actually have sex, whereas before it felt more akin to masturbating in my own mind for two. Fuck. This is how life is supposed to fucking be. Magic!

MEDITATION IN A NASTY PLACE

"He asked, 'What makes a man a writer?' 'Well,' I said, 'it's simple. You either get it down on paper, or jump off a bridge.'"[xiii]

Or maybe we can jump inside ourselves and see that everything is transient. Everything is moving. No matter the drama, the hardship, the anger—things keep on moving. Every moment is a chance to pierce into clarity. Every moment is a chance for greater understanding—and to understand is to forgive.

Meditation is difficult today. Extraordinarily difficult. At least, the idea of getting to my mat and sitting down with the turbulence that is coursing through my veins at this very moment is difficult. I am stuck in Taiwan, between a rock and a hard place. An idealist and a lover trapped between the greed and delusions of my family members. I can empathize with my father's position. I can empathize with my grandfather's position. I can understand and sympathize with every angry word spewing from my family members. However, I have no clear solution. All I can offer is my genuine presence and support, but it is indeed trying times.

"If you think you are enlightened, go spend a week with your family"[xiv]

When we are immersed in a nasty environment, it is very natural for us to resist meditation. Every fiber of my being right now is looking for escape. I want to distract myself with food, entertainment, sex, ANYTHING. The idea of diving into what is right now is simply unattractive. However, my past experience tells me that meditation is the absolute best thing for me right now. The knots and tethers of human interaction must be seen with clarity so that they may unwind. Emotional energies that are not seen and heard fully become fetters on our consciousness and can have deep and lengthy negative effects on our lives. The meditation teacher Thícht Nhãt Hanh says that in Buddhism, the forming of negative mental constructs and baggage is known as *samyojana*, and that meditation is the medication. It is 5pm now, time to sit; I will report back shortly my friends.

My practice just now was a bit different than usual. My breath was staggered and heavy. My palms pressed into the hardwood floor to support my spine, but all I could feel was the urge to slouch forward. The turbulence of my environment was weighing me down, and I gave in to the comfort of disengaging my spine and allowing my body to fall forward in a childlike manner.

As my head hung low, the anguished perspectives and voices of my family members began to swirl around me. I did not resist; I did not avert from the pain. I observed, and witnessed, and opened. I sought to be a lotus, at ease in muddy waters.

As I engaged in this practice, as I held the ideal of a lotus but trusted the process of the moment, a shift in energy began to occur. A strength, a light, a sense of clarity began to arise from within. My heart and head began to buzz with a different energy. An energy of clarity and understanding. The energy of the present moment. The energy of potentiality and possibility. My spine naturally became erect and my mental environment began to brighten. All we have is eternal now, and it is what I do with the present that matters most.

To repeat: No matter the drama, the hardship, the anger—things keep on moving. Every moment is a chance to pierce into clarity. Every moment is a chance for greater understanding—and to understand is to forgive.

"UNWHOLESOME ACTION, HURTING SELF, COMES EASILY. WHOLESOME ACTION, HEALING SELF, TAKES EFFORT."[XV]

Ooh wee, I have had this idea of "*going energetically uphill versus downhill within*" for some time now. This succinct and content-packed quote from Thícht Nhãt Hanh is exactly what I needed to see. You could say uphill energy is wholesome, while downhill energy is destructive. We could even get more technical and mention that many meditation traditions don't see destruction as necessarily bad. For me, part of meditation has been about learning to discern energies within that are wholesome manifestations of healing versus energies manifesting from fragmentation and destruction. To break an egg from within, life springs forth. Meditation, generally speaking, is a stream flowing toward healing, interconnectivity, and harmony.

Through allegiance to truth, through self-mastery, through the constant practice of not deceiving oneself, through the constant practice of opening up to one's own darkness...we go through a certain period of internal growth that makes it easier and easier to exist in a way that is healing and wholesome. Wholesome and healing energy has an uphill battle in our world, externally and internally. For reasons that we are not going to discuss here, my experience—agreeing with the quote above—is that wholesome energy takes tremendous effort and practice.

Even accepting this kind of energy can be difficult, let alone generating it or living contently among it. Realized human beings can act as a mirror for you; sometimes the mirror isn't so great to look at. They say we accept the love we think we deserve…

They say it only takes eight weeks of practice of see significant changes in brain structure. They say our bodies, on a cellular level, go through a complete OVERHAUL every seven years. Start where you are, use what you have, do what you can. Meditation is not just relaxation; meditation wants change at the cellular level. At the paradigm level. Meditation doesn't want to just reduce your stress—meditation changes how you perceive stress. It transmutes stress. It digests and assimilates STRESS. It's just so fucking exciting.

500

At 500 hours of meditation, I had just left the restaurant industry. I was newly single after an intense relationship and had just left Vancouver Island. At this point I was fully recovered from OCD and had no obsessions or compulsions controlling me anymore, and I rarely experienced anxiety. I still lost myself to anger once in a while, but it was quite different. The personality that used to punch his own face and then the concrete for a sensation of relief was long gone. The practice of getting familiar with anger can make one see that it is almost never warranted or beneficial.

Another interesting effect for me was that music and dance became more intense and vivid. I felt like my ears got an upgrade. Furthermore, dancing became natural and ecstatic; music flows through you sober when you develop a meditative body. By this point my meditation was a mix of moving meditation and sitting meditation—my sessions were about twenty minutes (or a bit more) of each. It was becoming easier to just find peace and stillness among everything else.

At the same time, paradoxically, the urge to jump out of meditation screaming with mischief was also rising. Life was going well in general—but at the same time, I had no purpose. I was lost; just wandering with a slight grin. Meditation made me feel free and empowered but I still constantly asked the universe what the point of it all was. I had no career vision and I had no life vision. I cared deeply about everything but felt powerless. I felt a bitter indignation inside; it had always been there, but meditation was urging it to the surface.

With another level of comfort comes another level of friction. As awareness expands into light, so does the potential for darkness increase. There is much pain on earth, and I had no answer for the suffering of the world. *What is the point of all this?* I kept asking, even during moments of apparent happiness. I stared up into space constantly. I kept meditating. I was smiling but apathy was growing inside me. I started whispering to myself smugly that I would not give a shit if I didn't wake up tomorrow. That summer, I was diagnosed with lung cancer.

A MEDITATION ON A MULTI-CULTURAL HAMSA

I was sitting on a bench in Germany when I saw what looked to be a multi-cultural ancient symbol. It was a Hamsa, a Middle Eastern symbol modified to include elements from a variety of cultures. (I invite you to Google search the following terms to get an idea of what I was looking at: Hamsa, Ba Gua, Eye of Ra, and Flower of Life.)

The interweaving of ancient wisdoms has been very useful in my personal life. The ancient wisdom practitioners, the ones I resonate with, seem to be uninterested in creating followers. They want to nurture us with autonomy and equality. The real teachers show you where to look but don't tell you what to see. All these traditions have so many parallels. They teach simple foundations of consistency and self-honesty. The simple but often ignored Golden Rule is always mentioned as well.

Milarepa, a famous Tibetan meditator, said his religion was not deceiving himself. His lifelong practice was to not deceive himself. Does that sound a little wild and overly simple but unbearably true at the same time? It sure does for me.

It is amazing the mental acrobatics we can all do. I am physically clumsy, but my mind will do a triple fucking axle and rationalize anything if I wish to do so. That's why meditation is so incredibly exciting. We go beyond the mind.

When we find a little quiet in our minds and we are quiet in our minds we might find we are not quite our minds.

That is what they say. That is what I've experienced. But don't take my word! Play with your own experience! Follow your highest excitement without hesitation—but at the same time, cull the expectation of what you think should be. That is the paradoxical balance we train for in meditation.

TATTOO MEDITATION

What would a tattoo meditation look like?
Explore with me?

The needle is about to pierce my skin and my notepad is ready!

The artist is currently working on my right shoulder, so luckily I get to sit upright. As I type these words I can feel the needle whirling against my skin. I breathe in with concentration, I find that connection with my breath that I've cultivated for the past seven years.

OUCH.

Near the armpit is tender. But the breath adds a certain sweetness to the experience, if I don't resist so much. The pain is real but I am aware that I am adding layers of intensity onto it as a result of unskillful mental activity.

I focus on my breathing again, and the breath anchors me slightly into the present moment. My awareness intends to pierce as deeply into right here and now as possible. I am opening my body to the needle through gentle mental guidance. I breathe. Ow, that spot is gnarly. Apparently it's called "pulling a line." The artist says she puts in a lot of work finding artistry and purpose in every line she pulls.

They say when you know how to listen, the guru is always present. Many meditation traditions believe in a high teacher within.

In meditation, our intent is listening. Exploring and investigating without judgment. Concentration without expectation is the name of the game. Every little mundane or sparkling stone is to be turned. Every little line in our story has depth waiting for you to explore.

I am still amazed at how expansive, deep, and intricate our consciousness is. The funny thing is that you can get along in life without digging too deep. Just beware that many people live their lives disguising fear as practicality. Nothing is quite as searing as the fire of regret.

Ow, this spot hurts.
  It also tickles at the same time.
  Awkwardly enchanting.

Breathing in, I open my mind to the pain. I want to run into reality. Breathing out, I am aware I am breathing out. Breathing in, the needle buzzes loudly in my ear. Breathing out, there is peace even now. It started with a doubtful open-mindedness seven years ago, but as I practice living, I believe. I believe there is peace if we choose to find it. There is magic for those who seek it. We need darkness to see the stars. The lotus blooms in mud. Even with the ink needle pricking me, I can see that there is a little room for peace. There would be a lot more if I was more skilled.

Never forget that in meditation we seek to raise our words, not our voices.

You must master a new way of thinking before you can master a new way of being.

RECOLLECTIONS ON GENEROSITY

My second teacher, Guru Chen, an artist and medicine man, taught me about generosity. I watched how he lived for many months in the countryside of Asia. He was a marvel. He had a commanding presence, but it was empty, mostly void and space. This meant his presence was felt but never imposed. He emanated energies of love and understanding. He was a true nurturer of the human condition. People from all over town came to see him daily.

Guru Chen has given me many extraordinary gifts without thinking of anything in return. He gives fully in that moment. All his love and desire for giving are sealed away in that moment and then it is forgotten. Happiness is found in trained simplicity. He doesn't hold on to ideas of his own actions—he does something, and it is done. The moment has dissolved. His attention does not hang on to the unchangeable past. He does not waste energy.

I remember one evening, after meditation and Qigong, he asked me to practice generosity. He said it was very important. He didn't say much else. I didn't feel overly inclined to ask why, despite feeling intense resistance to the idea in my gut. *He is just gonna speak in riddles anyway....so what, should I just follow the urge to give without abandon when it arises? What if this guy doesn't deserve it? That girl doesn't deserve it. I don't have that much to give.* I was caught up in my own mind again. Judgments about myself and others were the foundation of my reality. It was a manageable existence, but hardly free or joyful.

Guru Chen's short words have a habit of imbedding deeply into my psyche, so I played with the idea. I doubted its usefulness, but kept it in contemplation. I began to notice whenever resistance would arise internally with regard to giving. Whether it was sharing food, saying thank you to the bus driver, making a bigger gesture, or wishing a stranger well, I attempted to witness fully. I noticed resistance all the time. Resistance borne of fear, imagination, or personal agenda. I made a note that the resistance was almost always based on bullshit. Fear has its utility in life—but it was out of place here.

"YOGA IS LIKE MUSIC: THE RHYTHM OF THE BODY, THE MELODY OF THE MIND, AND THE HARMONY OF THE SOUL CREATE THE SYMPHONY OF LIFE."[XVI]

So what can meditation do for you? Meditation can help you understand and feel the rhythm of your body on a deeper, clearer level. Music will move through you fluidly. Digestion is improved. Sleep is improved. Recovery time is improved. Memory is improved. Creativity stirs freely. (The list goes on...but explore meditation yourself, forget advertisement.)

So what else can meditation do for you? As described in the above quote, with meditation you become more familiar with the melody of your mind. Through concentration, awareness, and an exploration of potential, we become familiar with how melodies are manifested, empowered, or disturbed in the mind. We see patterns. We gain insight. We gain spaciousness and equanimity. We gain control through paradox. (Forget my words, forget my mind, go listen to yours.)

Finally, what can meditation do for the soul? Not everyone believes in a soul, so let's just play around with the idea a bit. In my experience, a soul, or what I intuit as the soul, is happiest when there is alignment in our intent, thought, belief, and action. Meditation guides our consciousness to scan for alignment within our whole being. Alignment occurs naturally through awareness. A deep change in belief leads to a change in behavior. Insight manifesting internally rather than digested externally is MAGIC. The rhythm of the body, the melody of the mind, and the harmony of the soul create the symphony of life. It's your symphony to shape and mold. One note at a time.

If meditation affects the symphony of our life as a whole, then what is meditation here and now? Coming from a place of experience, not authority: I would say meditation here is a concentrative awareness and nonjudgmental witness to the energy that we are emitting. Emanating. Leaking. Oozing. Radiating. There is more of a focus on the subtle aspects of our creator-ness here. Exploring ideas that our mood, thoughts, intents, and emotion affect something possibly perceivable in the physical world. Meditation here is still an opening up. A conscious breathing effort. A curious attitude is always helpful. No doubt negative self-talk will arise here (or at least it does for me). Meditation here is about taking responsibility for every little facet of your existence. You are the conductor, the orchestra, and the audience of your own symphony experience. How tiring! How exciting! What note are you playing right now??? What are you into? Do you appreciate mischief and discomfort? Do you prefer to contrast your musical notes or do you prefer repetition into trance? Are you bored? Do you want to change?

EVERYTHING DANCES

Maya Angelou says everything dances. Everything has rhythm. Your depression has a rhythm. Your anxiety has an ebb and flow; you learn how to control it. Meditation is going beyond control. We get bored of control...

Everything has a rhythm. The demons dab about with the dirges. The saints lament and scream quietly. The entrepreneur tangos with tactics and risk. The grass yields and folds, surviving harsh winters. Thieves sneak and swerve. The sick squirm. The strong support. And suddenly they switch roles. Dancing within the cosmic universal dance creates entropy. Flux. Impermanence. Change is the only constant. *Swerve.* Keep on dancing, whatever your dance is. Everything has two sides to create balance, tension, friction. All with their own purpose and message. Are you listening to understand? Or just to reply?

BIG SEAN

"I don't wait, I marinate."[xvii]

CONSIDER THIS: Meditation is not necessarily about relaxation. This explains why Dr. Wayne Dyer says there is no such thing as a bad meditation. If I can make an analogy, think about going to the gym. When we go to the gym, we just go to the gym and start with the weights we can lift. We don't spend our time getting upset with ourselves when we can't lift 200 pounds the first day. I mean, even if we did get upset we would move on pretty quickly, because it would be silly to focus on such a thing for too long. When we go hiking, or when we go do yoga, or when we play rugby, we don't generally expect to be experts from the beginning, or give up so easily.

I very often see the perseverance of the human spirit—it is a daily occurrence, and everyone is hustling, even if it's not obvious, or agreeable. So just remember, meditation is about starting where you are and doing what you can. Any sort of energy directed toward yourself with an intent to understand, expand, and familiarize is good! Just like any weight you lift at the gym will go toward training the body, any conscious mental activity or breathing will go toward the net effects of a mental or spiritual discipline.

With exercise we can make our bodies savage, functional, and beautiful. With meditation, we can expand our consciousness, increase the depth and width of our field of awareness, and increase our ability to tune into the present moment. Even after seven years of practice I am still in awe of how deeply one can pierce into the present moment. It feels like I am barely scratching the surface. Meditation is a very broad word, with lots of layers of possible meaning and implication. So we can start simply: sit down, engage the body in a relaxed way, and seek familiarity with the breath. Allow yourself to be anything, but pay attention. Pay attention without grasping or judging. Any amount of time is beneficial, any degree of concentration is well suited, and any experience is appreciated. All states of consciousness have something to teach us in meditation. Just open up! Find teachings that make you curious and follow the path with great honesty. Discard what does not serve you. Investigate that which does not agree. Add what is uniquely your own.

MAKE MIND CIVILIZED, MAKE BODY SAVAGE

Tire the body so the mind can stretch out. Strengthen the vessel and find power in vulnerability. Temper the flesh and expose the core. Physical fitness is a great aid to a meditation practice. Do not deny yourself a healthy life. Commit to GIVING yourself five minutes after every workout. You sit, you engage, but you relax. You scan the body. You allow the mind to express. You give thanks to the body.

Even when your meditation is over, you carry your meditation with you. You carry your meditation and it gets lighter and lighter. You eat with appreciation. You drink with purpose. You walk connected, awareness in the present. Sometimes you drop it but somehow it finds its way back to you. You are a wave out of the ocean. You are the universe expressing itself as a human being. You yield to the unknown but you are firm in your roots.

VALENTINE'S DAY

Happy Valentine's Day everyone. Meditation, for me, has radically changed the way I give and receive love…

A few quotes for your consideration:

"Give love and then forget you gave it"[xviii]

"Act without expectation"[xix]

"Wisdom is knowing I am nothing, Love is knowing I am everything, and between the two my life moves."[xx]

It's interesting, to say the least, that almost every scholar of meditation and consciousness comes back to us with similarly-themed messages. Messages full of paradox and contradiction, designed to pierce those open to receive. We are all open to receive…the question is, do we give a shit? Are we motivated? Honest? Open? Or are we guarded and apathetic? If we are, that's okay—just get so intimate with the "negativity" that it has to change due to understanding and familiarity.

Back to the idea of love…I used to think I would run out! But all these teachers and guides kept telling me to play with ideas of love being infinite. Love is the substratum of our awareness. We always have the ability to give a loving presence if we dive into the moment. This was something they believed without exception. This is something they believed with conviction.

So I practiced doubting and contemplating their teachings for a long time. And I concluded that they really do seem to be onto something. Even in the depths of winter, I open myself to the idea that, as Camus said, within me may lie an invincible (and eternal) summer. I do believe it.

Everyone deserves love. Even the demons. Forgive my directness—I hate to sound preachy, I just want to express freely so that I can further my understanding. See, everything we do, we do to ourselves. It has been said that "If you truly loved yourself, you could never hurt another."[xxi]

Love is the universe supporting you in any way you choose. Love is the universe that watches you with compassion when you decide to enter a tough situation. Love is the awareness that wants to intervene but simply witnesses as you tumble and fall. Love is infinite. Love is boundless. Love does not mind the barriers you have put up against it, but it is always knocking. We always have a choice. You start with yourself.

A MEDITATION ON TRANSFORMATION

Studying quantum physics as a layman, I have come to understand there exists an aspect of reality that is completely interconnected.

It is my contention that through meditation, through the development of non-judgmental expanding awareness and concentration, we can tap into this aspect of reality that demonstrates our connectivity. The more we become familiar with this aspect of reality, the more life seems harmonious and magical—even amidst great suffering and corruption.

We can do this through an inward transformation of consciousness as a result of meditation training. Through deep recognition and insight in meditation. Doing all this from a center of complete personal autonomy to allow an experience of interconnectivity to manifest. Through all these things, the world cannot help but change. All of this starts with simple honest meditation. Face yourself and walk inward while holding the ideal of non-judgment.

This is an inward revolution where we all deeply realize our connectivity. Slowly, the idea of them vs. us becomes less and less manifest because it has no choice but to diminish. We have trained our minds to tap into the frequency of consciousness that KNOWS we are all connected. Somehow, it becomes natural—one day you find yourself more interested in understanding your enemy than judging or conquering him. One day, you find yourself still the same but completely different.

One day at a time, the world will change. All it does is change! With meditation, we can transform along with it. Stay in alignment internally and in harmony externally. We can ride the crazy surf of life only if we run *into* reality. Meditation is only concerned with what is; don't *imagine* light, *bring* light to your darkness instead. Non-judgment is light! Give it to yourself!

CARNIVORE

"I contend that this world does not need more monks in caves; this world needs more wizards in the city."[xxii]

I am a meat eater. I am a carnivore. I enjoy eating the flesh that was once a living, sentient, feeling animal. I just finished eating some food from the butcher across the street. Before I cooked the flesh, I held it in front of my body and closed my eyes. I thanked the meat and, with a sincere but clumsy heart, tried to acknowledge the suffering it went through. While cooking the meat, I opened to the idea of generating further gratitude toward my meal. I then practiced a form of eating meditation: I ate the food with concentration and conscious simplicity while kneeling in my meditation room.

Before the age of twenty, my diet was mostly meat. The only time I was eating things other than meat was when the food was enhanced by not being *just* meat—for example, a triple hamburger. I shunned vegetables and starches in general, aside from hamburger buns. I was quite overweight in my youth and relatively puffy in my teenage years. For as long as I can remember, I have craved meat. I remember being very young and becoming totally enamored with the street cart fried chicken get-ups around my hometown of Yi-Lan, Taiwan.

After the age of 20—after the onset of my journey of personal practice and cultivation—my dietary habits began to change from year to year. My perceptions around food continued to change yearly, as I participated in the experiences of autoimmune disease, cancer, and diseases of the mental kind. It has become quite obvious that taking care of this physical body is important if we want to truly say that we are trying to live this life to the fullest.

Excuse me. I digress. *Swerve.*

I have studied food from as many perspectives as possible. Through meditation, my tongue is no longer my master. I have weighed the issue of morality and the ethics of meat eating for a long time. I am aware of the atrocities and inhuman cruelties committed upon animals on a daily basis in the modern world. Still. I eat meat. I take as much as I understand I need and I try not to take more. My allegiance is to truth...and the truth is, at this time, I eat meat.

THE MECHANICS OF MANTRA

There are many dissertations on mantra meditation at our fingertips. Whether through books, teachers, or internet resources, if we want to explore mantra it is easier than ever before. However, there is nothing satisfactory about the practice unless we apply a visionary can-do attitude with regard to mantra as a form of meditation. Mantra practice, along with meditation in general, is a divine but slow-blooming seed. It is easy to get mired and euphoric on the way. Tumble and titillate, upswing and downswing. One day you may be in love with your mantra practice, and the next you may be ready to sign an annulment. The key is consistency in practice regardless of external circumstance. It is just that little bit of extra grit and diligence that pushes you into the territory of genius. Mantra work is completely voluntary. Mantra work is something you can dismiss and forget about. You will survive life without mantra. Only the lucky ones choose to find the time for mantra.

Putting the mystical, spiritual, or even subtle factors of mantra aside, let's talk about mantra in a physical way. If you will spare me the mental energy, please imagine a circle or a sphere. Allow this circle to represent your personal consciousness, your field of awareness. This is the space where your thoughts arise and manifest (and the more you meditate the more you see the difference between thought and the field where thought arises). Now, imagine a mantra, a mind tool, being inserted into the circle. Suppose the mantra is *Om Mani Padme Hum*, one of the most common mantras in the world. (This mantra is associated with the Buddhist figure Avalokiteshvara—but today I am most interested in communicating mantra to someone who doesn't have any interest in Gods or Deities. Mantra today is just a mind tool, and some people even create their own. A mantra is simply a physical, concentrated sentence, designed to access all the octaves of sound.) The mantra is now being injected inwardly at your discretion. We are sending energy into our personal field of awareness. It is a piece of energy, a wavelength, a signature, a frequency, floating and derping around in your consciousness. Spiraling conscious thought-created energy is being sent into yourself, by yourself, so that you can explore yourself. You create the mantra and send it toward yourself so that your field of awareness can be stretched, penetrated, and transformed.

So we take the mantra, and we run it in our minds with a gentle type of vigor and concentration. Depending on lineage, tradition, and culture, mantra chanting may be allocated to special times. Here, however, we are encouraging the practice at all times and as often as possible. We are looking to develop a center of peace, a familiar resonance within ourselves that we can look to regardless of circumstance. Whether we are eating, sleeping, walking, or fucking, we try to maintain the mantra. *Om Mani Padme Hum, Om Mani Padme Hum, Om Mani Padme Hum.* Yes, you will drop the mantra all the time, but that's okay, it won't break.

The mantra is applying a certain subtle force to your life. I see the seeds of genius in mantra, even if I see it as nothing but a physical sound tool. How you see mantra will evolve as you practice and dedicate some mental energy to it. It starts out simple (too simple—you may feel like it's akin to staring at a rock). However, the mantra is constantly exerting energy into your field of awareness, pushing into the space between your thoughts and expanding the imagined boundaries of your consciousness. The mantra calls on you to be present in the moment, unrelenting to complaints regarding circumstance. Training you and calling to you to come closer and closer into the present moment. It is a physical sound anchor that you resonate with. Mantra is the physical sound and reminder that is always trying to push you into the present, deeper and deeper. It is stretching your mental boundaries, illuminating conditionings and patterns of thought that don't serve you. The mantra practice does all this with a simplified sort of genius. Mantra is powerfully transformative yet easily overlooked and rationalized as witchcraft. My words are hopeful pieces of energy asking you to take a second look.

With practice, the mantra is gently buzzing underneath all the phenomena you presently experience. An argument with your Mom has whispers of *Om Mani Padme Hum* between thoughts and trappings. A walk with your lover has hints of *Om Mani Padme Hum* dancing underneath your feet. A discussion with your mentor has *Om Mani Padme Hum* swirling underneath your words. The mantra is asking you to step up your attention. Expand your awareness and focus your concentration. The effects of mantra are slow to become apparent but are nothing less than profound. Transformation beyond imagination.

It is a practice like mantra that can give you the personal insight of knowing that you yourself are master and student in one. Commanding a gentle work order while still exploring as a student is a keystone of meditation and practices of self-cultivation. This is your domain and no one can come inside, for better or for worse. This sword you command known as your free and sovereign soul can cut both ways, and no one has access to the hilt but you. You came into this world alone, you will leave this world alone, and the mantra is yours to access, command, and investigate on your own. Some will simply dismiss. Some will adopt blind faith. My personal experience is that the most satisfying path is one of personal investigation and discernment combined with surrender and commitment. Be skeptical and faithful at the same time. Entertain practices while submitting to them; realize you are much more than your mind.

This short essay is in no way a complete explanation on mantra meditation—in fact, it is nothing more than a whisker on the head of the lion. Mantra work and the understanding of mantra is a personal art and science. It is a journey within a journey in a largely intangible realm of thought and investigation. Be your own master. Dismiss that which does not resonate, but maintain the practice of opening up each day. Your personal answers will come when you develop the ears to hear. Work on your ears; let the messages come to you. Focus on the simple and the doable in this present moment.

TRADITION

Many traditions will say that you cannot have true meditation unless you have entertained a certain position of mind, a certain posture, or a certain experience of consciousness. Then again:

"Tradition is the illusion of permanence"[xxiii]

Nothing is permanent in this world. I am extraordinarily careful with absolutes, but this is one I have investigated internally and externally time after time and it does seem to be true. For now.

If meditation, a tool that can take us to the frontiers of human transformation and potential, is to stay useful, then it must adhere to the conditions of what is. There is genius in teachers of the past who gave teachings based on the unique conditions of their present moment—but consciousness is fluid and constantly changing and this makes transmitting meditation effectively a constant challenge. It is a pleasure to ride the surf rather than carry the load...but I digress.

Swerve with me to your internal landscape. To speak to an aspect of meditation, we may be interested in finding the space between thoughts. Although many may come to meditation seeking relaxation and "peace," what you might find is something altogether transcendent—if you can begin to find your feet on the conscious path inward.

What seems to facilitate our ability to fully explore our own consciousness is the use of a few keys: non-judgment, expanding awareness, and sharp focus. As our field of awareness toward life becomes more illuminated, as our faculties of focus edge toward laser precision, our chances of digging into the secrets of our own mind become facilitated. Most importantly, to be able to swerve in this process with a total lack of attachment paradoxically paired with passionate involvement will reveal a natural inner transformation. You can bring these key elements of meditation into all aspects of your life. It's volunteer work. Are you in or out? The journey is epic. The struggle is real. The fruit is ambrosia and beyond taste.

Relaxation can be bought. Meditation cannot. Seek meditation. Seek truth. Relaxation will come on its own. Relaxation will bore you and at the same time be with you as you begin to see the frontiers discovered from meditation.

FUCK OFF WITH THIS WHOLE MEDITATION THING RIGHT NOW PLEASE

Meditation is the last thing I want to do right now. I feel so much resistance toward the idea at the moment. All I want to do is sit around like a sloth or do hoodrat stuff with my friends. Neither of those options are really available right now to me at midnight here in Yi-Lan, Taiwan. FUCK! *Swerve!*

I have had an extremely stimulating but exhausting day. I have experienced all the extremes of emotion today. I am writing at this moment, not for your sake, but for my own. I am publicly announcing my commitment to meditate before I retire for the night. It doesn't matter how I feel. It doesn't matter what I am thinking. It doesn't matter how much my body and mind whine and whimper at the idea. I am going to meditate before I retire for the night. No matter the condition, there is a conditionless whisper toward meditation. A cosmic dance in the Hridayam is constantly beckoning to us, say the yogis. Will you come listen, seeker? Will you dance the universal dance without expectation?

The Zen tradition says: You should sit in meditation for twenty minutes every day, unless you're too busy—then you should sit for an hour.

If I DECIDE I am too busy to meditate, then I am essentially saying that developing and evolving the relationship I have with myself is not at the top of my priority list. As you know, I am a monstrous advocate for self-love and gentleness toward the self. I am not here to promote feelings of guilt around meditation; that's a common pitfall. At the same time, it is important I develop discernment. Tonight is a night when the strings of my being need to be tightened so that resonance can occur.

I can DECIDE right now that I would rather lie in bed and eat crackers sloppily while crumbs rain on my chest. I can DECIDE right now that I am too busy, too tired, too restless, and too wired up for meditation. I can DECIDE right now that I can always just practice tomorrow. I can delete this piece of writing and never post it. No one would ever know. The world will keep spinning and the birds will keep chirping…but I will know. I will have to rationalize my laziness. I will have to rationalize why I deserve to just take a break today. We human beings have the extraordinary ability to rationalize anything if we CHOOSE to. I'll just talk myself into believing I have more time. ("The trouble is, you think you have time," says Buddha.)

I am going to meditate before I retire for the night. I know it is the catalyst for evolution and the self-actualization I desire. I am going to meditate before I retire for the night. I know the inward action of meditation is the essential processing, digesting, and integration of today's fantastic and somber events. I know from experience that it is when I am most resistant to meditation that the practice is most powerful. Keep it simple. Keep it playful. Keep on keepin' on. Start where you are. Use what you have. Do what you can. Breathing in, I am aware of in-breath. Breathing out, I am aware of out-breath. I can feel how tightly my mind is grasping onto existence right now. There is no better time than now. There is no better place than here.

Lokah Samastah Sukhino Bhavantu.

THE ESOTERIC ANTENNA

I rarely get to speak with Dr. Tang, my first meditation teacher. Sometimes, I get to hear his more personal thoughts on humanity. Because he's a heart surgeon and the head of a cancer clinic, it can be surprising to hear him say that energetically, human beings are like antennae. He says that we are transmitters and receivers of energy and consciousness. He says that it is intense personal cultivation and development that allows our energetic antennae to resonate with less-known frequencies of the universe. It is interesting how such an educated man, with two PhDs in modern science, working within the materialist model of science, can still maintain a certain esoteric awe for life.

"The world is full of magic things, patiently waiting for our senses to grow sharper."[xxiv]

Patiently waiting for our senses to grow sharper. Well, I do contend that meditation brings our awareness to more subtle aspects of life. I do contend that meditation is the journey from the gross to the subtle. I do contend that through a softening of personal projections, our senses have room to become sharper and more developed. But magic? What do you mean by magic, Mr. Yeats?

“And those who were seen dancing were thought to be insane by those who could not hear the music.”[xxv]

Is there always music playing? Is there an equanimous tune we can learn to access in all situations? Is there grace behind suffering? Are seeds of light always present in darkness? Where am I going? What is the point of all this meditation? Huh?

Sometimes, when my body has been worked to the bone… sometimes, when my mind is tired of hearing itself…I fall into a space of meditation. I hear music that I did not have ears for before. I see subtleties my eyes did not pick up before. I feel frequencies my body could not touch before. I breathe in the scent of potentiality and transformation. I taste thoughts from inspirations previously unknown to me.

In meditation, I let go of the need for answers. In meditation, I embrace the unknown. In meditation, I rest in uncertainty. In doing so, I am moved to the realm of awe and curiosity—a place where magic is possible.

LET'S TALK ABOUT LOVE AGAIN

This meditation piece borrows some of my less-mature writing from April 7th, 2011. After about three years of meditation, I was beginning to gain insights into this idea known as Love. The insights came subtly, one by one. Gaining the insights was a little bewildering, and applying them and integrating them is even more so. A lifelong practice, I am sure.

I've always been a romantic. I believe I have an unrelenting thirst for experience and stimulation—adventures of all kinds beckon to my personality. I've always enjoyed the extremes of emotion. I like the movies I make for myself to act in.

I used to think love was something to be earned. Love was something only given to those deserving, and my standards were simply impossible. Looking back now, I had constructed a fortress barricading myself from love. Relevant Rumi says our work is not to find love but to destroy our personal barriers against it. I played judge, jury, and executioner in my head and gave out nothing but skulls. Once in a while I found someone who deserved love and would then give it, only to soon find the person could not maintain the bar of perfection I demanded. Love was something precious—and you only have so much to give away, right? I feared I would run out of love. Better hold on tight!

As I applied truthful contemplation and meditation, my personal relationship to this grand idea called love began to transform. Slowly I discovered that Love is to be given freely. Love is vast and limitless when I ALLOW it to be. When I find the courage to give Love without fear, I feel inner peace. When I can give without the fear of not receiving in return, I find that I receive more than I ever thought possible. The universe responds to the vibrations I emit, and when I am able to let go of my personal idea of how things should be an awe-inspiring harmony begins to spiral into reality.

How do we do this, though? How do we really live in this state? How do we actively progress to this point? How do we even see that this is a better way? Because, to be honest with you, if I had read something like this four years ago I would have cursed at the cheesiness and seemingly blindly optimistic words of this piece of writing.

As my meditation practice progressed, so did my level of self-awareness. I watched myself with great tenacity. I began to entertain the thoughts in my head without necessarily accepting them. "I woke up from the hell of unquestioned thinking," as Byron Katie says. Taking time to direct my energy inward, I began to notice patterns and conditionings that were not serving me.

Every time I withheld Love, my ego would grin and revel in a sort of immature pleasure. This satisfaction never lasted and along with it came a sense of craving afterward. A sense of grasping for more would arise often after such actions. Even if I felt like I was in the right, a hollowness followed. Righteousness is a golden chain. I am not one to demonize the ego, as it does serve a purpose. However, the more I practiced meditation, the more I resonated with a craving to expand myself out of the insignificant insecurities of such a false center of thought and action.

Meditation gave me the strength to explore this idea of Love without abandon and without limit. As I polished and cultivated my personal lenses of perception, I began to see love in a mandalic way. Love was no longer on a spectrum. It wasn't the opposite of fear or hatred or even indifference. Love was an ever-expanding mandala of life force that made up the substratum of our existence. I saw that the universe loved me in a very transcendent way. The world gives me the freedom and abundance to believe anything I want. If I wanted to create an abundance of lack, judgment, and insecurity, I was given it.

Love began to flower in my life. Love for the sick. Love for the demented. Love for the evil. Love for the unjust. Love for the malicious and ignorant alike. Brief flashes of insight and clarity illustrated that Love was an ever-expanding sphere of energy that I could empower if I chose to. It wasn't easy. I fell often. But if I fell seven times, I committed to standing up eight. I wanted nothing more than to fully explore and dive into this idea of Love. How sacred is it? How transcendent is it? How transformative can this force be? Step by step, breath by breath, intention by intention, thought by thought, moment by moment, I intend to find out.

"If the doors of perception were cleansed everything would appear to man as it is, infinite."[xxvi]

DISNEY'S *FROZEN*

I rarely get immersed in movies due to my explosive nature, but this film really spoke to me. I really do believe that when you know how to listen, everyone is the guru. Every moment in your life is a beck and call to something you wish to resolve within. The problem is that we can be very unconscious to the fact that this moment was, always, in some way created by us. To repeat after Carl Jung: "Until you make the unconscious conscious, it will direct your life and you will call it fate."

When we can watch and appreciate a Disney movie without labelling it as a kids' show, we can learn from it. When we see everything as equal, when nothing is below us, even the most childish choruses have divine details we are missing. Simple but difficult lessons of unconditional love are often portrayed in animated films. Perhaps unconditional love is something hard to believe in in our current times. However, as always, we have a choice.

We can choose to take a risk! Yeah, RISK! We can choose to hold the ideal of unconditional love but trust the human process of drama and desire. We can choose to see that all people, in some way, are seeking love, acceptance, and understanding in their own way. Their ways might be twisted. Tangled. Unconscious. Even malicious. But we can choose to believe that everyone is just trying to find a little internal equanimity. That feeling of contentment and ease that can define our lives...we all want it so desperately that we can become completely unaware of the daggers in our thoughts, words, and actions.

I am guilty. That is why I practice. I see how easily good intentions turn into the road to hell. I see the grandness of consciousness and the vastness of the unknown. I see the deep depths of the unconscious within me. Try again, fail again, fail better.

DR. TANG

My very first meditation teacher. I had an awe-inspiring meditation session with him at age 21 and the rest is history. *Swerve!* Some people just walk into your life and change everything with a snap of the finger. With a whisper of his realized consciousness, my life path forever changed for the better. Without his teachings and transmissions, I surely would not be writing to you today. If I say or do anything helpful, it is thanks to the seeds of consciousness given to me by this wonderful man. Some people—you are just indebted to them forever and yet they act as if you owe them nothing. Besides, there is nothing I can give that my teacher does not already have. The very least I can do is pay his blessings and goodwill toward humanity forward. Thank you, Dr. Dennis Tang.

EGO

The ego is simply a function of the mechanical mind. A natural creation of the human being in response to the world. A natural manifestation of wanting and planning in a world without guarantees. I cannot blame anyone for seeking solidity in a world of impermanence and flux.

Cease the demonization of the ego. Cease the demonization of your process. For it is in the extremes of judgment that we create ropes of self-bondage and self-limitation. We find hints of freedom and light when we can PERSONALLY see the value of process over product. I emphasize the word personally because there is a harsh difference between knowledge in the brain and insight in the heart.

Some studies have shown that the average human adult thinks between 50–60 thousand thoughts per day. Furthermore, studies have contended that almost all of us think the same 95% of thoughts. Or, more precisely, even if the thoughts themselves are slightly different, 95% of the thoughts manifest from the same old conditionings and belief systems. It is time to embark on the path of self-knowledge. Ask yourself and then answer yourself, over and over again. To keep balanced you must keep moving. To keep moving you must become your own master. A master with complete accountability and autonomy.

The path to freedom is jagged and full of obstacles. You will encounter guides and teachings, but ultimately only you can free yourself. PAY ATTENTION—are you giving your power away? Only you can see your personal process so clearly that you can create an opportunity to go beyond. It is your personal, wild, and powerful subjectivism that you must harmonize with objectivism. Only you can decide what is truly the next best step. You decide what to listen to. You decide what to believe. You are hypothesis and result in one. The observed and the observer in one. Marble and sculptor in one.

With complete autonomy and accountability, you bear all the fruits. You bear all the scars. Most of all, you get ALL of the lessons in each and every moment…stay present and you will go far.

IF I WERE A NONSENSICAL LION WE WOULD HAVE A ROARING CONTEST

A roaring contest…
Let us have a roaring contest.
A roaring contest…
Let us yelp and howl in protest.
A roaring contest. A roaring contest.
Looking loud and feeling primal, let us have a roaring contest.
A roaring contest. A ROARING CONTEST.
When the ego is crying we can have a roaring contest.
A roaring contest. A roaring contest.
Shout and scream in a roaring contest.
A roaring contest. A roaring contest.
What good is a roaring contest?
… … … .SHATTER YOURSELF.

THIEF OF SUFFERING

One of the greatest lessons I have learned so far as a meditation facilitator is not robbing people of their suffering. It is the ego that demands every session be spectacular, tranquil, and full of revelation. It is my challenge to give people the freedom and the strength to tumble. It is my challenge to make friends with failure and constantly reframe my personal ideas regarding "success."

Essentially speaking, meditation is much less concerned with right and wrong than transcendence. When we can tap into higher forms of consciousness through stillness, we naturally spiral upward with insight and integration. It is important that we become comfortable without condition. Rest in restlessness, unaffected by uncertainty. The less concerned with turning left or right we become, the more chances we procure for consciousness to naturally rise. Balance the wings of concentration and awareness, and soaring becomes NATURAL. True meditation is effortless.

I contend today that the keys to this natural evolution of mind, body, and soul are freedom and honesty. Give yourself the freedom to fail. Give yourself the freedom to fall. Give yourself the freedom to be unabashedly and honestly you. It is through magnificent sovereignty and autonomy that we shed the layers that hold us down. "You cannot rip the skin off the snake. The snake must moult the skin."[xxvii] Give yourself the catalyst of transformation. Meditation. Mindfulness. Autonomy. Complete self-honesty. Complete personal accountability. Self-mastery. OWN every little step of your journey, especially the cruddy parts.

"To be yourself in a world that is constantly trying to make you something else is the greatest accomplishment."[xxviii]

Own yourself completely. See yourself holistically. Investigate all aspects of your being with consistent curiosity. Open to the idea that there are countless vantage points and perspectives you have yet to uncover. A Zen mind is a beginner's mind. Begin with me again and again. One foot ahead of the other.

IT ALL COMES...

The mind, it is not designed to stop thinking. Your meditation is not expected to be pure, containing only silence and stillness.

You are the eternal reactor. Through cultivation you become the responder. Through insight you become the eternal witness…and then what? *What if I disappear? The rope that ties me to my idea of self is becoming frayed and ratchet.* Don't be afraid, the rope is not essential, things don't stop moving. Don't you know by now?

YOU can let it all go and it will still all get done

The mind thinks without your stress

The tongue salivates without your stress

Physical wounds mend without your stress

The body digests without your stress

Romance appears without your stress

Aging occurs without your stress

Death comes despite your stress

"You are standing on a bridge watching yourself go by."[xxix] Be that extraordinary watcher. I've been missing things. Still am missing things. Will continue to miss things. Practice, practice, practice.

Don't convince yourself that the world needs you to hold it up on your shoulders. Don't try to be a hero. Don't try to "get enlightenment." Just be as extraordinary of an ordinary human being as you can. That is enough work! I promise you—that is enough work, to allow the whole range of humanity within you to manifest in a compassionate but sovereign way. That is a life's work if you choose to believe in it.

Swerve! They say hell's road is paved with good intentions. You will crush yourself (you'll prove me wrong first #swerve). In your journey to become it all, you will crush yourself, and collaterally, crush others. Without consciousness, we hurt others. Without consciousness, we betray others. The paradox is that we rarely find the patience to hear some things if we haven't done some crushing of our own. We are Creator, Sustainer, and Destroyer, ALL IN ONE. What a PACKAGE we are!

THIS is what Lao Tzu is talking about when he says that by letting it go, it all gets done. You can let go and you will still be right HERE and NOW. You will do amazing things and none of it will have had ANYTHING to do with YOU.

DŪ

There is an interesting concept in the Chinese language. It is the verb "Dū." It is pronounced tightly and sharply, like how a mainstream rapper may imitate the sound of a MAC-10 as he recollects memories of life as a teenager in Compton. Doo Doo, Doo! Doo!

To have the ability to *Dū* someone or something is defined as the act of bear hugging in honour, WITHOUT CIRCUMSTANCE. Literally translated, you are hugging up or wrapping up something with honour, no matter what it is. It is speaking about the capacity of a being able to not only endure friction from others, but to find the honour and joy within the friction. To find the meaning of the friction. To find the capacity to understand and pull pain into your peace at will.

Rarely is this word used in a colloquial context. Generally, it is mothers and fathers *Dūing* their kids. It is religious and spiritual figures (if you aren't atheist) *Dūing* humanity. It is Mother Earth (if you allow personification) simply witnessing the atrocities happening above and below sea level. Rarely is it talked about in a colloquial context. It might even be perceived as arrogant to say that a human being has the capacity to *Dū* something or someone without wanting something in return. The Psychology taught to me in university in 2006 stated that pure altruism is not possible—I wonder if the books still sing the same tune.

Well, I dare say that meditation leads us to developing the ability to Dū things. They say maturity is the ability to understand why someone hurt you rather than retaliate. I say, through meditation, we develop the CAPACITY to understand something hurtful and not feel the need to retaliate. With meditation, we raise our capacity to Dū things.

In meditation, we work with and playfully train our personal subjective field of awareness. As we work on it (with a variety of practices that can be explained), our personal center becomes bigger or more well-identified. When your field of awareness feels like 100 acres instead of 10 acres, the ability of mosquitoes to annoy you is changed. However you want to look at it, I think long-term practitioners will agree there is growth and evolution in consciousness that is best defined SUBJECTIVELY. My ethics and logic teacher in University taught me that subjectivity is a dirty word (and on a somewhat unrelated note, she got in a spectacular way a few years later)—but the discussion of objective subjectivity in meditation will have to be discussed another day.

EXTREME EMOTIONS

On the meditative path, we might find we naturally pledge a certain casual but lifelong commitment to truth. Anything that is not in alignment with our highest beliefs and ideals falls away. We discover that love and potentiality are the substratum underneath all experience. We are sovereign beings with feet in our shoes; steer yourself like Seuss—HOWEVER you choose!

So perhaps you arrive at a place where you choose to live a life of love and truth. You hear words like "break your heart until it opens" and you feel a resonance inside. You decide that everyone is fighting a hard battle and that there is enough hate and criticism in this world already. You decide to discover for yourself whether or not love is truly limitless. You investigate for yourself and you fall seven times but somehow stand up eight. Love heals all. Love is the all-encompassing spiralling energy that can transcend and transmute hatred. Love is an endless well that we have attempted to formulate and control in our personal journey for fulfillment. With meditation, our plans start to fall apart. You might find yourself smiling in the unknown...

But what of extreme emotions? I may have discovered a certain sense of tranquility and equanimity internally, but

I still yearn to be as much a part of this world as possible. Meditation is running into reality. So when reality becomes a storm of emotion, negative or positive, I try to open. Open, open, open, and then open some more.

In the most extreme emotional episodes, I feel a teetering between personal ego and the infinite witness. I may tear up and howl at the moon, fully allowing my personality to express. I may beat my chest and sing until my throat is hoarse. At the same time, there is the watcher; the seemingly formless sky that contains the mountain peaks and clouds. I am on a bridge watching myself go by. I am perched up in love and understanding, witnessing myself go through life. Everything I am experiencing is the result of doing EXACTLY what I have felt like doing at every precious moment. The storm may be powerful and tumultuous, but it can't touch me. I am much more than that. Every moment is a gift.

"EVER TRIED. EVER FAILED. NO MATTER. TRY AGAIN. FAIL AGAIN. FAIL BETTER."[xxx]

This phrase is incredibly relevant when it comes to maintaining a meditation practice. We should expect obstacles in all aspects of life—but when it comes to meditation, in my experience, get your fail boots on. Come on, it'll be neato!

Meditation is about not only learning to fail, but even becoming intimate with the idea of failure to such a degree that you transcend it. Before I float off, what I am trying to say is that failure is not only to be expected in meditation but, in my personal experience, it is required. The mind must fall on itself and see its own shortcomings until it is ready to open and say: *What's next?* But before that, we must remember:

YOU CANNOT FORCE YOUR MIND TO BE CALM.

The active non-action that we learn to find in some styles of meditation can be very tricky to understand and, more importantly, internalize. The writer of *The Alchemist*, Paulo Coelho, says without action, there is no learning. This is very true when it comes to meditation. Every time you sit down to meditate and the rational mind comes in saying:

"I can't do this. This makes no sense. I don't get it. I can't get it."

That is a good thing!! You are learning what meditation is through exploring what meditation isn't. To go beyond the mind requires us to fully understand, embrace, and explore the limits of the mind. Meditation is unlike most things we do on a day-to-day basis in the modern world. The physical movement of our conscious energy is inward during meditation; we almost never do that in a wakened state. Stirring, shaking, or applying any sort of force does not help mud to settle and reveal clear water. When we practice meditation, we are learning to be affectionate, relaxed, and concentratively clear in our own space, without judgment. It starts out small, and baby steps will work just fine. What you will find is that this meditative awareness grows as you consistently apply conscious energy inward. What you will find in meditation is a sense of awe and openness to your own consciousness. It is the development of consciousness that allows your life to change in the blink of an eye: through seeing from a brand new vantage point that was not previously conceivable internally.

Meditation is the slowest-blooming flower I know of. Give yourself time, love, and consistency.

LOOK AT ALL THE WAYS WE CAN CONNECT

Before I got into meditation, the operative theme in most of my thoughts was disconnection. Aside from my inner circle, the world was to be judged and analyzed. I bought into an idea that said the best way to live is to create a bubble of manageability and expectations. Meditation, however, wanted to teach me something else. Meditation naturally tended to turn my awareness toward exploring ideas of interconnectivity and impermanence. It's very common for thoughts to arise without end in meditation, so it can be beneficial to hold ideas in contemplation for long periods. And, back to the idea of interconnectivity, I realized that meditation helped me build the mental fortitude to connect with everything. When your own waters are clear, or at least not murky and raging, you have the spaciousness to truly entertain this world. In return, the world entertains you. Look at all the ways we connect now. Sure we can talk about how technology can separate us, but at the very same time that same technology empowers human knowledge, potential, and sharing to a whole new level. They say enlightenment is intimacy with EVERYTHING. Everything. What a wild idea.

MEDITATION RECOLLECTION, THE FIRST 50 HOURS

Prior to meeting my first meditation teacher, I had accumulated around 500 hours of mental training in the form of EFT, ERP, and a variety of other cognitive exercises and therapies. These were the tools that allowed me to break free from OCD without lobotomizing drugs. Many of these modalities shared parallels with meditation. My first fifty hours of formal meditation was at age 21, when I received transmission and guidance from Dr. Tang, heart surgeon and meditation scholar. Meditation here was mostly a combination of a sense of confusion, boredom, frustration, and I-don't-get-it-ness. Meditation here lasted three to twenty minutes a day—mostly moving meditations, mindful walking and exercising, Tai Chi, Qigong, Kriya yoga, Bikram yoga, and mindful eating. Sitting meditation was incredibly rare at this time. Dominating thoughts were skeptical and self-indulgent. My mind was constantly finding ways to convince itself that it would be okay to just quit and go on to something else—that I had conquered my anxiety and OCD. My mind was "comfortable." *Why do I need to work on myself anymore?* the mind would lament. I tried to just observe the relentless complaints of the mind but at this point I could not yet discern between myself and my thoughts. I *was* my thoughts, and they generally overpowered me. My mind would always be jabbering during meditation: *Let's just go back inside, it's cold here, Matt's watching Always Sunny. Meditation is dumb—let's go play! You're hungry! Sleepy! Tired! Too excited! Rawr, I am a dinosaur!* In terms of benefits I did feel like I was at the beginning of an accelerated evolution but it felt incredibly hard to really give a shit and give it priority over immediate pleasure. I slept better…

MEDITATION RECOLLECTION, HOURS 50–300

The first fifty hours of meditation were done in a period of roughly three months. It was starting to become a consistent part of my life. I would notice on the days I convinced myself to indulge in laziness or excuses. I didn't guilt myself, but I noticed. (As meditation progresses, you might find that even guilt is sort of an indulgence, an escape mechanism of the ego.)

Hours fifty to three hundred of meditation were certainly interesting. I was starting to really notice benefits. Aside from the physical benefits (which you can readily find with Google), I remember smiling randomly more often. I remember moments of anger and intensity that had an extra sense of spaciousness to them, doorways to insight and transformation. I found it easier to go to the gym every day. I found it easier to recover after binge nights. I felt less alone in social settings because the fragmentation within was starting to make sense. The first fifty to three hundred hours of meditation probably took me to age 22 and a half. But I am laughing here, because meditation to me then was still mostly moving meditations and applying teachings of mindfulness when it felt natural to do so. My sitting meditations would rarely last more than five minutes. Five minutes felt like an eternity. Staying moving to appease the mind was sort of a theme. That sounds pathetic to me right now, but that was the truth. Life and meditation during this time was about appeasing the mind. Working with the mind. Distracting the mind. Playing and exploring with ideas of mind. Control. Change. Malleability. Potential.

By this point I'd had a few mystical and shamanic experiences unexplainable and inconceivable to my Canadian-trained skeptical, rational, scientific mind. I enjoyed them and found them to be curious and sometimes beneficial but generally kept quiet about the subject, internally and externally. I had stopped going to Bikram yoga due to philosophical differences and was mostly meditating outdoors and often at a small mountain called Tolmie in Victoria. Sometimes I even met a few friends for meditation on this mountain. They were always interesting experiences.

MEDITATION RECOLLECTION, HOURS 300–500

At age 23, I was at roughly 300 hours of formal meditation practice. At this point, my most common meditation routine was hitting the gym then heading to the top of little Mt. Tolmie right afterward to do Kriya yoga and sitting meditation. At this time I was generally comfortable sitting for about fifteen minutes before I was overwhelmed by the march of machines in my head.

During one sit—it must have been around July—I was feeling super-elated and content all at the same time. I was seeing past my own layer of bullshit with clarity for the first time. I started to notice that everyone was fighting a hard battle in some form or other. My perception was gradually changing, and thus my experience of life changed. I got in touch with ideas of sonder (the realization that each random passerby was living a life as vivid and complex as my own), impermanence, and interconnectivity. At the same time, studying meditation, the mind, and the science around it all made me realize the more I knew the less I knew. With regard to consciousness, a part of me was shrinking while another part of me was expanding; it was magic. As a wise man once said, "Wisdom is knowing I am nothing, Love is knowing I am everything, and in between the two my life moves."[xxxi]

At this time I am steadily approaching 500 hours of practice. I have difficulty communicating to others what meditation is. I have a hard time defending meditation and explaining what I am doing when I'm just sitting there breathing. However, the effect of the practice on my life has been simply astronomical. From day one it was changing my life financially, emotionally, mentally, physically, and spiritually. I was transforming at the paradigm level. I was not changing my thoughts; I was changing the field of awareness from which thoughts manifest. Meditation was the catalyst for the personal transformation that I desperately needed. I was starting to develop a new paradigm of life nurtured by meditation and truth-seeking. However, my early practice lacked love in many aspects. Wisdom and intelligence untempered by love and compassion can lead you to dark places, and I was not done learning from the negative principles of life. And the thing about meditation is, the more you do it, the less possible it becomes for you to lie to yourself.

BRAVE MEN DON'T SLAY DRAGONS, THEY RIDE THEM

With all this talk lately about making friends with your demons, I think this idea (paraphrased from an episode of Game of Thrones) is very relevant and frankly glorious as it relates to meditation. You know those movies where the hero learns how to ride a dragon or some other amazeballs mystical beast? Well, in a sense, meditation feels like that. I have learned how to clumsily and brutishly ride my inner space tiger. If you want mastery over something else you first need mastery over yourself. A beast cowers to greater power and preys on weakness. But stillness and tranquility, well, maybe that will make the beast curious. Through self-mastery, self-honesty, self-compassion, self-curiosity—and some discipline slash playfulness—you can find your still-point. Your gap between thoughts. Through practice, you become the gap. The infinite spacious potential of your being. If you frequent the internet you might see the common story about how human beings have two wolves inside them—one is all the perceived negative mental states and the other all the perceived positive mental states. Meditation can take us to a place where, while we understand the interplay of the negative and positive principles, we can act beyond them.

RIDE YOUR BEAST

SILENCE IS BETTER THAN BULLSHIT

TRANSPARENCY EXERCISE

I would like to do a transparency exercise today—perhaps it will be useful in illustrating my inner landscape after approximately 2500 hours of practice with a variety of teachings. My brain is a bit scrambled, so this is a good exercise for me as well. Meditation is linked to self-preservation, even if we see that the self is impermanent; in meditation we are always working to expand our consciousness and field of awareness to be more capable of digesting paradox.

All right my friends, let's begin:

My body is sore, so my posture is slightly sloth-like. Zen traditions might hit me with a stick right now, but I'll just focus on some softer teachings, ha! This meditation will be a mix of awareness and concentration, Vipassana and Samatha. I notice my brain is foggy and my breath is more stagnant than usual. Breathing in deeper, I scan my field of awareness. There is a sense of fear and guilt. *I should not partake in such heedless activities.* I stiffen my posture. A quieter whisper manifests and says that every experience has a lesson. Ahh, the mind can rationalize ANYTHING. Breathing out, I try to make a connection with my being rather than just my brain. Breathing in, I am unobstructed by thought. Breathing out, *ooh that is nice*—haha I am focused on words again. Breathing in…breathing out. Breathing in, a variety of emotions and judgments arise. Breathing out, I greet them with a clumsy wink. Breathing in, I am breathing in…it is okay to just exist. Breathing out, I relax but I feel a certain vigor arising borne of understanding. Growing old is a privilege denied to many. My eyes feel energized. Breathing in, I am aware of the breath in. Breathing out, I expel all that is untrue. Breathing in, I listen intently to words rooted in love. Breathing out, I affectionately study thoughts guarded by fear. Breathing in. Breathing out. Breathing in, I trust the process but hold a vision. Breathing out, I seek comfort within uncertainty. Breathing in, my posture energizes. Breathing out, my whole being energizes. Breathing in, I wish to stop writing so I may continue. Breathing out, I wish you all a wonderful day. Thank you for joining

"ALL I CAN DO IS BE ME, WHOEVER THAT IS"[XXXII]

This quote could be the subject of a meditation. It could even be seen as somewhat of a mantra, even. The quote also contains the flavors of a Zen koan: self-questioning with a sense of openness. This is certainly experimental, but as a meditation, I think we might get a little bit out of it. Who knows? *No guarantees but I'd like to proceed*, says the seeker.

We could take that sentence—*all I can do is be me*, *whoever that is*—and zero it into the present moment. Over and over again, we bring and that attitude into the moment and hold it while consciously focusing on our breath. Symmetrical posture, engaged core…I close my eyes and begin to loosen my intention with regard to control. Like Krishnamurti says, meditation can be a choiceless awareness. Now, the quote, the mantra—*all I can do is be me*, *whoever that is.* In this very minute, all I can do is be my tired self. The next minute—*all I can do is be me*—I am so overwhelmed and stressed and I can't meditate, but that is who I am right now…again, all I can be is me. The next minute…all I can be is my bored self. The next minute…all I can be is my restless self. *All I can do is be me*, *whoever that is*—it feels like I am being someone who can't meditate, and that is who I am. That's okay! All I can do is be me, and right now, I think meditation is a waste of time and I don't really get it. *All I can do is be me*—I am confused and frustrated, but I am just going to keep this idea of resting in uncertainty…that is who I am right now.

This meditation is an exploration of openness and the potential in every moment. I hope this post communicates that in some way. Keep exploring your own consciousness; be curious. Be your own master, be whoever you are, whoever you think you are at that moment. Moment to moment, intention to intention, thought to thought.

THE TASTE OF FEAR

You know, I taste fear every day. Every time I post a piece of writing, a piece of my soul, I feel the reverberation of creation. As I create, I feel the urge to destroy. Not good enough. Not fresh enough. Not true enough.

You will tell me when my words are stale? Darling?

You will tell me when my message has become stale and garbled?

Dear reader, will you do this for me?

Slap me with the kiss of truth?

I feel I have been too hasty lately in my writing. I feel my communication can be better. I want to talk to you today about meditation and fragmentation.

One foot ahead of the other. In meditation, along with the development of discernment within, I began to embrace fragmentation. The more I saw my own process, the more I saw fragmentation. I noticed how chaotic and murky my inner landscape truly was. The practice of awareness and non-judgment, however, led to an internal alchemy, a process of transformation. Starting around the third year of my practice, every time I sat down in meditation I could sense something subtle and grand was going on. I focused on the ordinary and held onto nothing.

Stay honest. Stay diligent. Stay curious and playful.

The focus is on the process, not the product. You pay attention, but at the same time you are relaxing into it. You are learning to push and pull at the same time. Harmonizing opposing forces within is part of the practice. For me, it felt like there was intense processing of energy all the time. Pay attention. Notice the manner in which your thoughts manifest. Pay attention. Play with the idea that there is more to know about yourself. How vast is consciousness? Pay attention. Pay attention. Noticing how the brain fires in reaction mode versus response mode. Pay attention. Pay attention. You are a very fragmented young mind. The very least you can do is pay attention.

Using my personal vices as an example—if you desire to be reckless and unwise, then own it and make it sacred. Honest. Truthful. Find truth in mistakes. Find truth in unruliness. Find truth in fragmentation. From fragmentation, to compartmentalization, to integration. Meditation is the catalyst for transformation within. Simple breathing. Simple focus. Simple concentration. Simple experiencing. Make the simple sacred and the miraculous follows naturally.

As you progress on the meditative path, you may find that you start to feel more spacious within your own skin. The pathways that your five senses fire upon become more clear and resolute. Exciting times, my friends! Glory awaits you. A sense of smoothness develops as the meditative cloth sandpapers away untruths. To repeat my past self: With a new level of comfort comes a new level of friction. With the expansion of awareness comes the increase of both light and darkness. Learning to stay balanced as power and intensity increases is one of the many fun challenges on the inward path. Only you can feel it. Only you can experience it. Only you can be the true master.

"THE JAPANESE SAY YOU HAVE THREE FACES. THE FIRST FACE, YOU SHOW TO THE WORLD. THE SECOND FACE, YOU SHOW TO YOUR CLOSE FRIENDS, AND YOUR FAMILY. THE THIRD FACE, YOU NEVER SHOW ANYONE. IT IS THE TRUEST REFLECTION OF WHO YOU ARE."[XXXIII]

In psychology, there is the idea of the Public Self, the Private Self, the True Self, and the Ideal Self. Many cultures and schools of thought speak of this separation of consciousness and how we only allow certain aspects of ourselves to manifest in relation to our environment. I would like to quickly reinforce the idea here that meditation is the allowing of *all* aspects of consciousness to freely manifest. But, back to the image above, the idea that we all have three masks is very interesting when discussed with regard to meditation. *Swerve.*

The first face exists to protect us and to assess risk. To feel each other out in this dog-eat-dog world. (My editor is quite adamant about me explaining what the other two faces might mean to us, but she and I will have to happily disagree here. Discover your internal landscape for yourself. Make your own labels. Emit your own intention completely into your life so that you may know it so well that one day you can let go of all that does not serve you.)

From what I understand, many meditation practices seem to encourage the merging of the three faces, and this has been true in my experience. I can confidently say that who I am when I am alone is quite close to who I am when you interact with me in the world. They say you teach what you most need to learn...and seven years ago I would say I had gigantic chasms between and misalignment in my three faces. They did not exist in harmony—they opposed and contradicted each other. My conscious landscape was fragmented, schizophrenic, and infertile. I was unable to integrate life because of the disconnection and fragmentation within. Unable to plant truth because of acidic soil. How can anything but suffering manifest in such an internal landscape??? This is what I say to myself after seven years of practice: How could I have expected a joyful life when the internal environment that I dwelled in was discombobulated at its foundation?

This is not to say that it is not okay to have privacy and secrecy. Not at all. The point here is that we want to create an internal landscape of harmony and alignment. It is said that happiness flows easy when all aspects of consciousness are in alignment. Alignment doesn't mean anything here except a congruent picture of truthfulness flowing forward. Meditation wants your first, most public face to be like your third face—for it to be as pure of an emanation of your core being as possible. Meditation wants to bring out all the celestial individuality we have within out for sharing. In whatever manner you so choose.

TODAY'S MEDITATION: JUST SAY HELLO! :)

There is a form of cognitive behavioral therapy known as ERP, or exposure and response prevention therapy. ERP has been shown to be very effective for treating OCD and other anxiety-based disorders. As I study meditation, I have found that ERP is, in many senses, a meditation on our fears and our "flaws." This is a highly transformative practice. So, if you would please join me in today's meditation, let's just say hello! We are looking to open up to ourselves and we aren't really interested in anything except that. Taking an active but restful position, we can begin with a few deep breaths.

As your breathing settles, begin to approach all phenomena, both internal and external, as valid. Whatever comes up, just say, "Hi!" No judging, just acknowledging. And notice when you instinctively want to invalidate something. That knot in your neck? *Hello! You aren't the most pleasant but you are here for a reason, eh?* That anxiety and discomfort in your solar plexus? *Greetings! When did you get so big? Sorry I have been ignoring you!* Your roommate walking around loudly banging pots and pans? *Hail! Please continue to live freely ;).* That happy memory that pops up when you try to meditate? *Hey! Nice to see you again! Is there something I haven't learned from you? I mean, you keep visiting!* And finally, that scary spiky ball of fear that you keep out of sight that also rises to the surface during meditation? *Well hello! I was hoping you would just disappear, but I guess there is a reason I am seeing you. What's up??? :)*

BEFUDDLED MEDITATION

I awake at 10:30AM with a semi-vicious hangover and bike my way west of where I live, toward the trees and University grounds. I find myself outside of Aphrodite's Cafe in Vancouver and sign myself up to wait forty minutes for breakfast.

It is a quaint and earthly cafe with a tree directly outside its front door. After five minutes of jacking around with my volatile mind, I get the idea to meditate. (Perhaps it is the sudden awareness of ants crawling on the tree that allows me to hear the wisdom of nature. Every corner of our existence is brimming with life—test it.)

I ask for a spare chair from the two diners enjoying brunch outside. I sit down, keys and paper bag in my left hand, headphone wires twangled up in my right. It's strange—I feel immediately pulled into the deeper depths of my consciousness, though all I am doing is applying non-judgmental focus and awareness.

Altered states of consciousness seem to manifest easily after seven years of meditation. Choosing to be choice-less in front of this cafe, opening up to all the noise around me, I find myself in a state of light trance at noon in public. Giving up the need for peace, I find my awareness tunneling into still but vibrant aspects of my consciousness. My breath elongates naturally and I take pleasure from a sense of rejuvenation for thirty minutes. By the end of my meditation, I feel completely energized. *Goodbye hangover—always a pleasure!*

I press my knees into the concrete as I say goodbye to the tree. I feel eyes on me as I do this, but I could not care less. It is a simple duty to show gratitude for my particular connection into nature today. Connecting with nature deeply means connecting with myself deeply. I did not come into this world, I came OUT of this world—a wave out of the ocean.

"MAN CANNOT REMAKE HIMSELF WITHOUT SUFFERING, FOR HE IS BOTH MARBLE AND SCULPTOR"[XXXIV]

This is one of my favorite quotes and, like many things, makes me think about meditation. Let's do a morning meditation together.

Breathing in, I bring my awareness to just me. Breathing out, I give myself permission to be a bit selfish.

Breathing in, I expand the fresh air of today into my body as deeply as possible. Breathing out, I intend to let go of all which that does not serve me—but I will be affectionate toward myself if I cannot.

Breathing in, I take full responsibility for the energy I bring to every situation. Breathing out, I hold strong in my core and am ready to leave any situation that does not resonate with my highest truth.

Breathing in, I welcome challenges and take ownership of them, knowing deeply that it almost always takes two to tango. Breathing out, I affirm my life is mine to shape—I am the master of my fate, I am the captain of my soul.

Breathing in, I am aware I am breathing. Breathing out, I let all the happenings of the world inside me and outside of me to just express freely.

Breathing in. Breathing out. Breathing in a bit deeper. Breathing out a bit more slowly. This is a new day…I wonder how it will unfold???

A FLASH OF RED

I admit it. I lose my temper much more often than I think is acceptable. We celebrated my Mother's birthday today and I have to begrudgingly admit that I really lost control for a little while this afternoon. One of my triggers was hit on the head with a precision blow. Memories and visions of violence against women...the injustice between Men and Women in Taiwanese culture...my personal baggage with my own traditions. Flashes of fiery red energy coursed through my body in an instant. Emotions surged and neurotransmitters swarmed; mindfulness shattered. FREAK OUT. I was screaming and punching inanimate objects; a child desperate for a cure. All I wanted to do was go nuts. Destroy things. A desperate but misguided expression.

Noticing the moment. Noticing the gap between thoughts, gaps between waves of negative emotion. I slip in. I fall into mindfulness. A sharp inhale. I am the sky again. How did Anger surge and consume me so fast? Hot red lightning. Spicy cinnamon tamale. Crackling, piercing, overwhelming energy. Fuck, it vexes me so deeply to see the strong abuse the weak. FUCK, I fell. I respond to anger so easily sometimes. I resonate with it without effort. I vibe with anger. I see the legitimacy in vengeance sometimes. Righteousness is indeed a golden chain: alluring.

The problem is, understanding the pitfalls of anger intellectually does not mean the body and/or the heart will cooperate. I have to admit to you that I succumb to anger. Meditation has not freed me fully from anger yet. Rather, I have yet to free myself. Many questions can arise with regard to anger and meditation. Do we stifle the anger or do we allow it to express mindfully? Can we be so familiar with consciousness that we can witness anger rather than *be* anger? Can we transmute the anger and channel it into something else? Is it just a matter of chilling out and moving on? Letting it be? Or letting go? Do we need to dig deeper? Or stop digging? How many times can I lose my temper a year and still look you in the eye and say I believe in meditation?

I am happy to be flawed. Happy to be learning.

SELFISH MEDITATION

Today's meditation is selfish. I am going to focus on my personal perspective: *Be here now. Freedom and equanimity is the substratum of this moment. Be here now.* I can remember times when I did not believe this. *Be here now.* What of men in chains and children in slavery? Tell me the grace behind their pain. TELL ME. . .! *Be here now.* Tell me something that isn't complete bullshit. *Be here now.*

Breathing in, I am aware of breath. I experience crinkling and cracking up and down my torso. My focus darts all over. Twist. Nudge. Push. Chew. Tangle. Breathing out, my body trembles as opposing forces clash within. My personal desire to harmonize and unclasp is clashing with energetic graspings. Oh, I am a human being and I want you to HEAR ME, whimsical universe! Do you tremble when I roar—or do the trees pity my unruliness?

I want to roar so loud that my stomach churns, but I cannot disturb my brother resting from his travels. Dear Andy, can you feel how my mind is SCREECHING with energy? *Be here now.* I consider the environment. How does my personal truth meld with the truth of the moment? I clench my jaw. Exhale. I am opening my mouth and contorting with exaggeration. Is there peace even now? I want to jump out of my skin! OORAH. Breathing in, I am aware of in-breath. Breathing out, I feel air exiting my body. As I remember the presence of mind to simplify, a shift in consciousness starts to percolate. Oooh, the bubbles of peace and tranquility; they are not unlike sparkling champagne.

Be here now. Oh just be here now, dear seeker. Yes seek with vigour—but also sit with your own mad stillness. Allow the world to carry you into its divine stream of flux and entropy. Impermanence, dear. Don't look back; you can't go that way. Yes, the mind contorts: But this, but that. This reason and that reason. This expectation and that expectation. Oh, dear seeker just be here now. Here is where you are. Now is what you have. Oh, dear one, just be here now.

A soft flash gazes over my consciousness and suddenly I have the giggles. The drama is drama is drama is drama. The internal battle is seen for what it is. My breathing is drama. My love is drama. My dream, my suffering, my stumbles, my stars. Drama. We're all just here dancing the dance of dances. Oh, just be here now. Come back to your heart center. Come back to you. Come again and again. Fail again and again. Be here. Now. Be the master. Be here now. You are the master.

"I HAVE NO SPECIAL TALENT, I AM ONLY PASSIONATELY CURIOUS"[XXXV]

Someone just emailed me asking for meditation dialogue. How do I stay honest? How do I really see things as they are? These were the sentiments of a sincere seeker looking for more clarity, truth, and peace in his own life. To be honest, I struggle to write anything useful here. There is no secret greater than consistency. There is no technique better than self-honesty. Yes there are many esoteric teachings and more difficult to access teachings all over the world, but there is no need to yearn for secrets. At, least, that is my personal opinion after seven years of practice and seeking.

The work is that it eventually leads us to seeking within rather than "out there." There is something to be said about exhausting our outer desires. Approaching our expression toward the world with mindfulness can help us find the doorway within. Exhausting the rational mind, turning all logical stones, and listening to intuition. Doing all these things in harmony without grasping is, in my opinion, meditation. You don't need anything except yourself. Be confident. Fall confidently. Be weird, confidently. Be confused, confidently. Own every aspect of your being. Bow to every aspect of your being. Make sacred every aspect of your being. And every aspect means *everything*—don't twist the words. Don't deny any aspect of yourself, at least in meditation. Best wishes to all of you today.

I SHOULD...

The mind and the ego. They are like children. Demanding beyond reason. Repeating without tact. *I should be here. I should be this good. I should I should I should.* Relentlessly insecure....

In meditation, we learn to nurture our awareness so that even these aspects of ourselves become channels for truth and joy. Don't demonize your ego; get familiar with it. Don't force the mind silent; allow the mind to become silent (don't hold your breath). The truth. The soul. The spirit. The higher brain. The heart. Whatever you identify as the highest point within yourself is quiet and confident. It's there, and it has always been with you. It whispers to you always. The question is, do you want to or know how to listen?

"Let go or be dragged," the Zen masters say. "What you resist persists," say others. Life is already complex without us adding to it. So don't make your meditation complicated. Don't let what you can do be blinded by what you can't do. When you sit down to meditate, stop judging yourself. See how hard it is to just experience yourself. It will make you go, "Huh? Why am I doing this to myself?" And then you inquire deeper within. Keep going till you can't anymore.

Give yourself a smirk! Stand up and shout, "I love you sweet universe, what a joy it is to just be alive with you! The darkness helps me see the stars."

THANK YOU TO ALL MY FANS

(This piece of writing was done online at a time when I just beginning to find my online presence)

I am blown away by the support, everyone—thank you. It's funny how we learn to find our voice in this noisy world.

The following meditation piece is all about nakedness. Meditation is feeling the fear and doing it anyway. Meditation is stripping down in a world that is constantly telling you to be a certain way—a world that tells you that to be something you must put this and that on. Meditation is getting naked and listening to the heart; finding freedom from within.

A voice in my head says that when everything is in place, I will find peace. However, my teachers whispered, find peace and then everything will fall into place. Meditation is not about being perfect—and boy, did I have the wrong idea about that. I pursued meditation first out of necessity, but then it became the practice of finding true freedom and liberation in every moment. I decided that I didn't want to ever make decisions motivated by fear anymore. And to break myself from fear, I had to strip down in front of my fears and invite them out for courtship. I had to accept myself where I was, even if I was not satisfied. I had to appreciate where I was so I could take the next stride with clarity. I held a vision but I trusted the process. Through my own murky waters, I started to learn how to look left and right at the same time. Up and down simultaneously. Seeking the middle way. Embracing paradox and contradiction so that I had a hope of freeing myself from duality.

"Righteousness is a golden chain," someone once said[xxxvi], and I used to hold onto judgments as if they granted me joy. Before meditation I waited for life to give me meaning. Now, I know this life is mine to create, for the benefit of all beings. I urge you to open up to the idea that there is more to you than your pains and pleasures. Look inside every day, embracing frustration and confusion. It doesn't matter if you're atheist, agnostic, Buddhist, Christian, or Jedi. If I can do it—if this idiot punk kid from Taiwan can do it—SO CAN YOU.

MEDITATION AND CREATIVITY

Today's meditation will be on creativity. It is very useful to meditate on the creative process and learn to see how it manifests in the seed. From beginning, to finishing, to sharing, to the final end, my creative process is bombarded with self-limiting thoughts. Why is that so? Is it the human condition? Is this something we all experience? I do think so.

Meditate with tenderness and tenacity on expression. That means be yielding to your inner expressions, give them space to be what they are, give them time to speak to you. For me, the greater the expression, the louder a voice says: *Who are you to speak your truth? Who are you to express? Who are you to share? Why is your message valuable? Who do you think you are??*...self-limiting and obstructing thoughts.

We all experience these. There is deep interconnectivity when it comes to the paths we all take toward self-actualization and fulfillment. We share many struggles. We bleed the same fear, we desire the same peace. The manifestations of that fear and peace may be different for each of us, but they share deep similarities in origin. When I allow myself to be free without judgment, naturally, this has to extend to those around me. If I do not extend to others what I apply to myself, the foundations will crack.

EXPERIMENTAL MEDITATION

I am going to make a little meditation tonight. This is slightly experimental. I am going to design the meditation in a way that hopefully creates a mental environment where it is easier for the proverbial mud to separate from the water, you could say. Many Zen masters describe a meditative non-action as the best action for gaining mental clarity. A common theme among meditation scholars and teachers is that there exists within us peace at all times. Or at the very least, there is an eye in every storm. And what once sounded absurd is now beginning to seem plausible for me after seven years of practice.

All right, so let's begin. I take a relaxed but engaged posture throughout my body and place my hands in a symmetrical position. I close my eyes and take a few deep breaths all the way into my belly and lower back. I let my breathing become mostly automatic but with a hint of effort and guidance. I notice the dryer is on again; it's loud and has a constant high-pitched whining, but that is okay. I open myself up to the idea there is a spacious peace within me. I look for it but I cannot find it, and that is okay. Taking time to meditate, I think, is utterly absurd, and that is okay. For some reason all this breathing is making my stomach knotty, and that is okay. I am feeling angry and restless at the same time, apparently, and that is okay too. My mind is going crazy—it's getting louder and more demanding—but this guy says it's okay??? Whatever. The dryer is so loud—what brand is it? I guess it's okay, though…but why do I keep investing my energy in hearing it fully? My legs are stiff and my shoulders hurt, but that is okay, this is my body and I better treat it good. My mind won't stop racing, I can't meditate…and that is okay? I am sitting here feeling silly and confused, and that is okay! I kind of enjoy just sitting here by myself, accomplishing nothing. This guy says I am doing much more, so I guess it's okay…does he really believe in this???

"MY RELIGION IS NOT DECEIVING MYSELF"[XXXVII]

I have given a few meditation workshops here in Vancouver, BC, and I find myself repeating one thing. I am always talking to people about Milarepa's famous meditation quote, in which he states, "My religion is not deceiving myself." WOW. What a religion. That's it, eh? Well I'm intrigued!

My seven-year meditation journey so far has been a constant shedding and moulting of bullshit. To backtrack a bit, I took a bunch of upper-level social psychology classes in University without knowing that they would not contribute to my degree. Village idiot for hire! (To be honest, my attendance in University was terribly poor but there was a girl I dreamed of asking out all the time in these particular social psych classes.) Synchronicitously, however, these courses were some of the most valuable for my life so far.

I remember learning that in terms of communication, we are not as smart as we believe and we are not as effective as we believe. Social scientists are finding that we as a species make a number of "mistakes" when it comes to perceiving and understanding each other. Paradoxically, we are also incredibly agile internally and able to deceive ourselves even to our own surprise. Sometimes we have no idea what we want or intend to achieve until the coin is in the air. At least, this is absolutely true for me. To speak like a punk: We're fucked, but it's chill. Even if this sounds grim to you, we are meditators—we believe anything can be changed.

To relate this quote to meditation, the practice here would be alignment. In life, we practice self-honesty and at day's end ask if we really walked our talk. In meditation, we witness things in our being that are not in alignment with what we believe. To further complicate things, oftentimes we don't even know what we believe. But things might seem a bit more fluid and malleable in meditation. Our sense of identity might begin to loosen if the anxiety decides to leave us. So we just keep watching. We watch for patterns and constructs of mind that lead us to true freedom. We watch for abstractions and conditionings of mind that no longer serve us. In meditation, we don't push, we don't pull. We witness. We metamorphosize.

WILD MINDS MAKE STABLE HEARTS

Wild minds make stable hearts. This little sentence came to me a few days ago and it keeps poppin' in my cerebellum. I hear it so often: *I can't meditate because my mind won't ever stop. I can't meditate because my mind is angry. My mind is restless. My mind is a rogue roller-coaster. My mind is an unruly unicorn.* Sorry to break it to you (and to myself), but that out-of-control mind that you think is so special and unique? We all have it. I've yet to meet someone who has found the meditation journey to be easy—but I can say with conviction that it is worth it, worth it, worth it. The crazy storm that is your internal landscape? It is your best teacher. It is a portal into so much more, if only you can help yourself look at it in a new way every day. It is the only portal you have. It's you. Honor it as it is. Your storms, your demon dens, your sunny nooks, your restless recesses—they are all sacred. If you can't see them as sacred, know that at the very least, they are all *you*. It is the liberating and tender ownership of all aspects of yourself that will continually guide you on your path. Next time you sit down to meditate, let it be! All of it. At least, this perspective was very helpful for me...

MEDITATION ON PUBLIC TRANSIT

I am in transit for about an hour and a half today and I seem to have misplaced my headphones. Oh. Big fuggin' deal. Alright. I am getting on the bus. The driver is a bit overzealous to say the least, but moving on. I sit down. The seats are very comfortable. In Taiwan all the buses have WiFi. I am in Vancouver though; my mind likes to warp around like a space doofus. I am sitting in front of two people. A young man and woman. They speak English while interlacing Mandarin words into their sentence. It's kind of novel, but I am still complaining.

Would be nice to have my headphones...go into my own world. If I had that, I would feel more peaceful and comfortable. Ya. As I experience this personality I am laughing at it. Silly kid. Is this present moment so horrible that you need to run away from it with headphones? Where is the peace and equanimity you believe is always accessible? Punk...wake the fuck up. A few shifts in perception occur and all of a sudden, I am peaceful. All of a sudden, my breath is expanding into the resistance in my being. My shoulders are no longer ajar and my face softens. It feels like all those hours I've spent meditating triggered some sort of sudden change in consciousness. It's like the non-judgmental awareness of the universe within me asked the tiny little insecure ego to let it drive for a while.

Among the loud noises all around me, I have found a concentrative stillness that I can harness. It all started with developing familiarity with the breath. My mental state is now relaxed enough that I can create this piece of writing. I used to be so deeply restless and anxious, even in pleasant situations. Angry and bullheaded to close ones. Overly analytical and fragmented in public. Now I can clumsily find peace and harmony often, it seems. I remember getting hints of this peace, even amidst cancer.

I don't think there is anything special about me. I just kept believing it was possible. My teachers helped me believe in human potential and transformation. I am not saying you should too. "Should this" and "should that" phrases often inhibit us more than nurture us…I simply hope that we can all remain curious.

"I WOULD RATHER BE SLAPPED BY THE TRUTH THAN KISSED WITH A LIE."[XXXVIII]

In life and in meditation, an allegiance to truth is a factor essential to our practice. We practice preference for the truth no matter how much it stinks, stings, or sucks. Life can already be incredibly difficult and it can be a relief to quiet the whinings of the ego through meditation. The ego is never satisfied. So we practice a choiceless awareness, as Krishnamurti describes. We practice being the sky and not the weather, as Pema Chodron describes. We train our consciousness to see things as they are rather than as we want them to be, as Dr. Wayne Dyer describes. We align ourselves to the truth of this moment, the truth inside us, and the truth of others. We allow the world to be as it is. We realize we are a wave out of the ocean. We learn how to trust in the unknown.

Rumi was a 13th century theologian and poet. His work is very commonly seen around Vancouver in the yoga community. To properly understand this loaded sentence, we need to understand Rumi a bit more. Rumi was, first of all, a deep Sufi practitioner. Sufi practice is mystical in nature and is a branch of Islam focused on self-discovery, self-mastery, and meditation. Meditation in this tradition often involves complex and even chaotic dance movements. The movements are repetitive but can vary from teacher to teacher. My understanding of some aspects of Sufi modalities is that they form a practice of liberating the mind through physical concentration and exploration. This essence of meditation can be found in a variety of other traditions all over the globe.

So, through self-realization practices, Rumi—the poet who sees with a mystical eye—says "Embark on the journey of love. It takes you from yourself to Yourself." (A similar line is found in yogic sutras but I digress.) Meditation, Yoga, Qigong, Sadhana, Sufism, Prana, Tao...they are all explorations of Love and Freedom in their own way. They are tools, techniques, philosophies, permission slips, manifestations of universal harmonies.

To stay on the topic of meditation, my experience is that although the technique may be simple, the practice is a journey of Love. What I mean by that is that meditation is an internal application of love to EVERY single facet of our being. This is not a journey you can finish in a fortnight. This is a journey that you will scoff at and then perhaps tumble and fall into. I fell. Over and over again. Everything within you that is not serving you, aligning you, empowering you will be exposed by practices like meditation. You are shining a light into yourself. You are committing to truth. You are cultivating your very own field of awareness. Through gentle, affectionate, and concentrative practice, the caterpillar morphs into a butterfly—without really ever "trying."

I've barely touched on what Rumi is packing in that tiny little sentence but it's a start. Be well my friends.

MEDITATION AND PERSONAL TRANSPARENCY

I have to remember. I am here to write about meditation. I hear a voice in my head. It says I am being repetitive. It says repetition is not special. It says I need to dazzle my readers and another simple meditation is just not going to cut it. Good thing I don't believe everything my mind thinks anymore! I don't have to buy everything my mind tries to sell me because I believe deeply in repetition. I believe deeply in the simple. It is the repetition of simple yet profound meditation techniques that transforms us. I am talking transformations at the foundational level of your being. Beyond stress and relaxation.

To swerve slightly, Aristotle proposed that we are what we repeatedly do. Based on that premise, excellence is not an act but a habit. We can make meditation a habit. The habit of finding freedom and empowerment in any situation. I did it while my mind played tricks with OCD. I am doing it now in a much more comfortable place. You can do it too; we are all special or we're all not. Either way, it's just between you and the universe. Meditation is just trying. You just have to want to meditate and you are already doing it. Your attention is placed on the realm of self-transformation and that is enough. Crawling in confusion on your hands and knees is not necessarily frowned upon in meditation. Yes, I get tired of trying too. When you're tired of trying, let yourself be deeply tired of trying. When that gets old, try again. Try something new. Fail again. Fail better. We can be born, we can die, and we can fall in love all in just one day. Our lives can change, too, just in one day. Every little moment, mundane or magical, is ever passing and never returning. Meditation is the practice of making the most of every moment. The paradox is that the practice, at some point, becomes effortless.

The time on the clock says 10:50 PM. Let's sit here until 11:10. At least I am going to. Feel free to quit at any time. It's okay to burn bridges in meditation. Another path will manifest. I am going to sit here, stare at the notepad app on my phone, and see what I produce. I will sit here and focus on the sensation of my breathing. I will allow my breath to expand and elongate naturally. I will allow internal and external phenomena to occur without resistance. I will attempt to become deeply involved in the moment while not being attached. If my bliss is interrupted by sharp noise, I will flow with time into the next moment. If my restlessness is interrupted by peace, I will listen to the sounds of silence without pressuring for an encore.

To go back to simple teachings; breathing in, I am aware I am breathing in. Breathing out, I am aware I am breathing out. I sit here and allow my mind to express. My mind is not the picture of peace and tranquility, but just giving breath to the idea changes my experience. I can feel the change of expression in my genes, or maybe I am just nuts. *It's been ten minutes. If I didn't have this virtual notepad in my hand I would be more peaceful.* Blah blah blah, boring complaints and imaginings of the mind. Consistent scumbag rascal my mind is, but I love it. I continue to make peace with my breath and my restless mind. I entertain my brain with quotes: "Be humble for you are made of earth. Be noble for you are made of stars."[xxxix] I continue to participate in the balance of meditation. We just keep trying to mentally digest and harmonize paradox. Keep trying to hug demons. Keep inviting your anxieties to come over and hang out. Breathing in. I am meditating. Breathing out I am meditating. Breathing in, I am. Breathing out, I am.

"JUST WATCH HOW OUR WORLD IS CHANGING HOW PEOPLE ARE CHANGING. YOU CONTRIBUTE EACH TIME YOU SHOW YOUR MASTERY OVER YOUR OWN CHOICES FOR THE ESSENCE OF YOUR BEING RATHER THAN YOUR REACTION TO THE ILLUSION."[XL]

Someone asked me today if it was normal to experience lots of negative emotions as we begin our meditation journey. First of all, thank you for asking...it makes my daily writing commitment easier to fulfill. Now, I am not authority on normality but from what I understand, experiencing fear, anger, grief, and other difficult emotions is incredibly common when we start meditating. I believe Eckhart Tolle says the hardest thing about meditation is your own personal idea of what it should be. It's very hard to sit down and not think that you are messing it all up. And you will—at least I did—but it's okay!!

First of all, directing a witness-like energy to ourselves contributes to our overall development. Furthermore, meditation can be an unfurling of the deeper recesses of our psyche. It is an intentional sinking into our subconscious. I don't know anyone who is without demons. So invite them out for a hangout sesh. No judgment. No pressure. Just hang out. Rock out with dirty socks on. It is impossible to have an experience with your demons and not gain something from it.

On another note, Pema Chodron takes on another useful approach. She says be like the sky, and know that everything else is just the weather. Now this doesn't mean you sit there pretending everything is all groovy. It means you are trying to approach your own human experience with a bit more depth, width, and capacity. Allow the weather to be as it is. And you, the grand sky, the field of awareness from which all springs forth, are the gentle cultivator.

"I MYSELF AM MADE ENTIRELY OF FLAWS, STITCHED TOGETHER WITH GOOD INTENTIONS"[XLI]

When I first started meditating, for the first three years I was constantly bathing myself in feelings of guilt: *I am not a good enough person for meditation—that stuff is for saints and holy men. I do not deserve peace because I got drunk and high last weekend. I am guilty because I lost my temper. I am guilty because I should have offered more of my time to the world. I don't deserve to spend time meditating and getting familiar with myself.*

Don't get me wrong, meditating for three years brought me incredible joy, growth, and clarity. However, in the back of my mind I would have this yipping noise asking me once in a while who I thought I was to pursue such high ideals... and I think this little self-sabotaging voice exists on a frequency that affects every one of us on Earth. It is the remnant pollution of old belief systems designed to limit us, not nurture us.

Meeting my second meditation teacher, an artist and medicine man who learned from Tibetan, Nepalese, and Taiwanese traditions, was a complete gift. His words and teachings were always encouraging. "Every saint has a past and every sinner has a future," he would gingerly say. He didn't absolve me of my guilt; rather, he held a space and helped me meditate until

I could integrate a perspective that allowed me to embrace my faults in a way that fuels me toward creating a brighter tomorrow. Thank you, Master Chen, you are one of many humble hidden gems on this earth, doing work quietly, sacredly, unassumingly.

OBSESSIVE COMPULSIVE DISORDER

I have been asked to describe how meditation has affected my anxiety issues, so here we go. I was diagnosed with obsessive compulsive disorder seven years ago and was prescribed SSRIs. I never took them. It was intuitive—it felt like a mental lobotomy. I refused to accept such a reality. So I struggled for about a year. Shit was really weird; when the mind gets so loud, it can drown out the communications from reality. I was obsessed with the idea that I was going to lose my mind. I had an irrational fear of going crazy and it was all I could think about. 24/7. All day. Every day. I would wake up and after about ten minutes my stomach would be fixed into a permanent knot. For some reason my mental alarm would not turn off. Every single experience of my life was tagged on with a question at the end: *So am I crazy?* For some reason, overnight, a switch flipped in my head and life became one big scary question: *Am I crazy?* Meditation was the only thing that worked. The type of meditation described in mindfulness traditions. "Running into reality" and "running into your fears"—those types of practices worked for me. I had to explore all my fears and get to know them well so that I can understand. Understanding is a key.

Long story short, the mental hell which affected me physically is completely gone. I dove into myself. Everything that made me panic—I invited them out at all times. I looked at them, got to know them, sang to them, and then laughed with them. Then they just disappeared into another form of mental energy. All that mental weightlifting I was doing propelled me to new heights of insight and understanding. The pain was 100% worth it. The pain came of me. I created it. At least, I co-created it. Through breathing, self-honesty, self-marvelling, and a little bit of unorthodox discipline, you can change your life. Beyond imagination.

My message, at the core, is that if I can do it, so can you. I am special, just like each and every one of you. I have survived many things, including domestic violence, thyroid disease, and lung cancer, but NOTHING was ever as debilitating and paralyzing as mental affliction. And it was just in my head!!! How could it affect me so? Why couldn't I just turn it off?

But ahhh...when you are quiet in your mind you will realize you are not quite your mind. Speaking candidly: If my laughter and joys are sacred, why aren't my demons? If I treasure my humor and sense of romance, why do I not treasure my darkness and anger? When I deny myself, I fragment myself. When I am fragmented, I suffer. My friends, I have only one message: If I can do it, so can you. If I can do it, so can you. If I can do it, so can you. Wishing you all joy, harmony, and most of all, clarity.

MEDITATION AND ENTHUSIASM

My dear friends, would it surprise you if I told you that meditation is a doorway to effortless enthusiasm? Someone once told me that there is no activity more miserable than trying to be happy. What we want is natural manifestation of happiness. Natural arising of enthusiasm or bust. Just sit and let things percolate. I contend that meditators and truth seekers are not willing to settle. We are after the simple yet sacred things in life that simply cannot be bought.

I dare not say I am invulnerable to apathy. Feelings of helplessness with regard to the plight of this world have always been a struggle for me. Dark nights of the soul are experienced by all seekers. Without a doubt, however, meditation has been absolutely magical when it comes to my general sense of exuberance and enthusiasm toward life. This is coming from someone who used to be able to find fault in fantasia.

Personally speaking, how meditation leads to enthusiasm exactly is a bit of a mystery. I want to unravel and unpack it for our mutual benefit and understanding, but there are no exact formulas for human potential and development. Yes, we can attribute it to physical changes in the brain but that would only cover a small dot on the mosaic that is consciousness and self-actualization. Meditation is the integration, evolution, and harmonization of logic and emotion. The tangible is alchemized with the intangible. The negative principle is merged with the positive principle. Union of dark and light, male and female, sword and sheath. Meditation is art and science in one.

The more I practiced stillness and non-judgmental awareness, the more I experienced enthusiasm borne of understanding. Insight sprouting from within is massively different than mere intellectual understanding. Through the embrace of the unknown and the negative, the radiance of life shines through. It is then we can truly feel and understand the sayings, "Life is already so difficult, how can we be anything but kind?" and "Everyone knows something you don't know."

The willingness to explore and embrace all the negative aspects of our world leads us to a wider perception of life at large. At this very moment there is countless suffering and injustice on this planet. How lucky I am to be sitting here in contemplation. How lucky I am to be exploring my own suffering in a comfortable way. Each breath is a motherfucking gift if you can see with eyes unclouded. The gates of our personal perception are to be observed (metacognition) and studied on a daily basis. COMMIT to yourself. As Rumi said, "Yesterday I was clever, so I wanted to change the world. Today I am wise, so I am changing myself."

Aside from the enthusiasm borne of understanding, there is enthusiasm manifested through spaciousness. The more we meditate, the more we discover spaciousness and potentiality in our internal landscape. We attain the ability to find tranquility and freedom in seemingly shitty situations. We develop a strong internal locus of control. We develop autonomy. Sovereignty. Complete responsibility. Everything is my choice, even in the most choice-less of situations. We develop a toolkit that allows us to become more involved in life but at the same time, less attached. It might sound like paradoxical bullshit, but keep practicing. As your internal field of awareness develops and expands, so does your ability to digest and harmonize conflicting forces. We free ourselves from within and along with it comes an enthusiasm for life like none other.

Finally, there is a more esoteric perspective with regard to meditation and enthusiasm. The more we meditate, the more our energetic centers (you might call them chakras) can interact with the world. The more I developed myself as an energetic being, the more I resonated with life in general. Attraction to the pure and natural aspects of life becomes ferocious. Absolutely magnetic. I am a moth flying to the flame of divinity; I am Larry's childlike exuberance. Subtle energies course through my body without effort, pulling me toward the sacred and the authentic. Sometimes I pass a tree and I HAVE to snuggle up on it. Kiss a leaf. Say, "Hello, dear tree, you are wise and intelligent beyond my scope of understanding. Thank you. I am so happy to be sharing this moment with you."

Honestly, my friends, it is a complete mystery to me. Meditation is a craggy pitfall-ridden road that has led me to an enthusiasm that seems to manifest naturally every day. This thirst for life is on another level; it witnesses the darkness of humanity but is not stained by it. Focus on the present moment; don't let the mind get carried away. Meditation is a focus on process over product. Take care of your personal process to the best of your ability. Rest when you need to. Cry when you need to. Be depressed when you need to. Own all of it with mindfulness and just trust your process.

Rumi again: “Keep breaking your heart until it opens.”

THE ENERGY OF TAIWAN

My good mate Paul asks: How does the energy differ when meditating in Taiwan? Does the experience change for you in any way? I gotta show some gratitude for this question—it's exactly what has been on my mind.

In total, I meditated for about 90 minutes yesterday. Shit was galactic. In one sense, meditation in Taiwan is no different. The action is gentle focus on the breath and non-judgmental awareness. The attitude is vigor harmonized with a willingness to yield. Playfulness alchemized with diligence. These are the staples of my meditation. Make the simple sacred so the extraordinary has space to manifest.

From another vantage point, meditation is completely different in Taiwan. The culture, conditioning, and upbringing of the people affect the energetic signature of the area. We are energetic beings. We can measure the effects of human consciousness scientifically. We can investigate the existence of subtle energies personally through hypothesis and experimentation. Meditation becomes a playful dance of seeing how our internal peace resonates or wrestles with our current environment. We are powerful sovereign beings; beseech your birthright. The subtle energies that I feel surge through my body are no longer a subject of debate; we learn to clearly discern imagination from reality. Chakras, Prana, Tao, Qi. Labels and constructs. Oh how the wonderful manifestations of humanity dance and dazzle.

My actions in meditation are the same, but the manifestation of my meditation is always unique. It's a new moment of spaciousness and potential. A new experience of equanimity and tranquility. I smile when I try to kiss the earth with my feet; how piercingly insightful awareness of the present moment can be. "Meditation is running into reality"[xlii] ...am I getting close? Meditation is the act of diving into the universe. A raindrop of divinity falling without preconception. Truth in stance, stillness in motion, merging yourself with the ocean... Meditation is hard work, but no one can be excluded. Find your way inward and you will know awe and gratitude anywhere, anyhow. Thanks for the question mon ami. Wishing you all equanimity and equality.

A POEM BY DANIEL F. MEAD

"If you would grow to your best self
Be patient, not demanding
Accepting, not condemning
Nurturing, not withholding
Self-marveling, not belittling
Gently guiding, not pushing and punishing
For you are more sensitive than you know
Mankind is as tough as war yet delicate as flowers
We can endure agonies but we open fully only to warmth and light
and our need to grow is as fragile as a fragrance dispersed by storms of will
to return only when those storm are still
So, accept, respect, and attend your sensitivity
A flower cannot be opened with a hammer."

If we approach our own meditation with the attitudes described in this poem, I think we could change the world. This poem is so great because it hits on the idea that humankind can endure and create unspeakable amounts of agony. But if I may be bold, what the world needs now more than ever is a softness borne out of understanding and wisdom. I dare not say I have it but I surely desire for it. I believe there is a unique flower or fire or imprint in each of us waiting to bloom fully. It is an exciting time to be alive, if I can just get out if my own way. If you are just starting to play with the idea of a meditation practice, read this poem before you sit and try to bring the essential attitude of this poem to yourself. Watch and observe where resistance arises in you. Make savage the body but peaceful the mind, says the samurai.

CANCER CHECK

I am in Taiwan, having just finished my fourth annual lung cancer checkup. I see that even amongst daily doses of laughter, dancing like a nymph, and optimistic mischief, I have been hiding away a cavern of anxiety and worry. A subterranean dungeon full of worrywarts, if you will. I did not realize how much stagnant energy was being processed in my subconscious until I got the news I was tumor-free. I want to say anxiety is negative energy, but at the same time it contains lesson after lesson. The seed of yin ("dark") is always in yang ("light") and vice versa, contend the Taoists. The depth and intricacy of human consciousness is simply staggering. "Sell your cleverness and buy bewilderment," urges Rumi.

As I walked into the cancer clinic I noticed a female monk meditating in the corner. Her energy was busy but not without beauty. I said hello and hugged the head nurse, a dear healer to me. She greeted me, smiling out loud, bearing teeth. She instructed me to wait by the windows. There were three chairs. I sat down in the corner, knees just a little weak. Shortly after, another monk appeared—male, medium build, smiley disposition on first impression. He walked right up to me and sat down next to me. I quickly learned he came to this clinic for Hepatitis B treatments. His energy field mixed with mine and I could feel his radiance. He was just doing some maintenance therapy, he said with a glimmer in his eye.

We chatted briefly and I found out he used to work in Phoenix, Arizona, until he left home for the Buddhist Monastic life at the age of 38. A Taiwanese monk was speaking to me, the only Taiwanese-Canadian in the clinic, in English. How sublime. I told him that I am actually extremely interested in meditation and consciousness. He told me his name is Jack.

We bantered a bit and shared our meditative philosophies. Resonance. "My religion is not deceiving myself," I said, quoting a famous Tibetan practitioner. "No shortcut is the best shortcut" he replied. As the conversation dwindled, our energetic interaction ramped up. Communication is largely non-verbal according to our modern thinkers, and at that moment I certainly would have agreed.

I found it extraordinarily easy and natural to sink into a meditative state with him. This happens often around consciousnesses that have been intentionally trained. I felt no pressure. No personal grasping. No objective. Just a state of natural progression and understanding. The vibe was warm. Shiny and spacious. I peeked at him and noticed he was doing some form of open-eye meditation. I closed my eyes again and the next sixty minutes blitzed by in a divine way. What would a medical clinic be if it did not test your patience?

I thanked him for the interaction and sharing of knowledge and he immediately thanked me back. I couldn't help but laugh; our eyes were on equal planes, there was no above or below. Goodbye Jack, it was an absolute pleasure.

With gratitude and anxiousness, I then found out I am cancer-free. One more checkup next year and I am considered safe. Admittedly, I needed the bitch slap of life that is cancer. Because of it, in the depths of apathy, I found light. Keep looking. Keep trying. Keep going. Ever tried, ever failed, no matter. Try again, fail again, fail better.

SPACE TIGER

"Be curious, not judgmental"

I think this line of thought is very useful to a meditation practice. Let us sit down. Any way you prefer as long as it is comfortable, relatively symmetrical, and engaged. Engage your body with ease…lower spine, upper spine, neck. If they are in a poor posture relative to your natural posture, correct them. Now we play with the idea of turning the energy of our attention inward. We can scan the body, we can draw more focus to the breath, or we can attempt to hold in our minds a wider landscape for all things to occur.

Along with the engaged but at ease physical instructions, the mind is to be guided in this same way. Let the mind do its thing. Become the witness of the mind and all its wonderful or treacherous manifestations. Is the idea of being curious about yourself ridiculous? Do you feel any resistance toward such an idea? For the next five minutes you could sit quietly and let all the happenings of your external world and internal world simply happen without judgment.

There is a sense in which we are trying to live the moment in an experiential way rather than an analytical one. Some would say that our minds, especially in modern times, are completely engaged in analysis for the majority of the time. So be curious, not judgmental. About everything! That's our meditation. While focusing on the breathing and keeping a restful yet wakeful state. Even a minute can be good. Gotta start somewhere. My mind used to be a space roller-coaster. Now it's more of a…space tiger.

TURBULENCE

It has been a particularly rambunctious and resistant two weeks with regard to my meditation practice. For a variety of reasons, I have found it a bit more difficult to stay in meditation for more than twenty minutes at a time recently. I have been feeling extra physical and explosive lately and my monkey mind seems stronger. It really wants to leap up and shout. Going inward and cycling down the gears of consciousness has been difficult lately.

Now, it is very natural and habitual for the mind to constantly creep around with nagging negativity. Even though I am vigilant against thoughts that don't serve me, I can still hear the whispers of the internal peanut gallery: *You've fallen behind. You're too guilty to meditate. You're too fun-loving to meditate. You just don't have the discipline.*

To stay balanced on the middle way that is meditation has been tricky for me. It is a lifelong practice. We must adopt a visionary perspective about the whole experience and then continually bring mindfulness to the process. I have had many dark nights of the soul and know I will continue to fall down when I least expect it. We must remember that as awareness expands, so does our own capacity for both darkness and light. Carl Jung said our leaves will reach heaven only when our roots reach hell. Intense isn't it?

We must develop a loving kind of trust with our own process. We must remember that although the universe is entropic and everything is in flux, there is an essence of self-organization to life. We can open up to the idea that everything is happening for a reason and smile when we can't see that reason.

We must witness our current situation with clear sight and compassion while trying our best. At the same time, we need to be able to loosen the tension when it is time to rest and contemplate in preparation for tomorrow. This is the divine play of the musical string; knowing when to loosen and when to tighten allows resonance.

The crux of this practice is flexibility in all avenues of thought and practice. A forty-minute meditation is not necessarily superior to a twenty-minute meditation. What is most important is our state of consciousness. Mindfulness is a non-judgmental way of witnessing ourselves with flexibility, authenticity, and self-honesty. It is when we bring mindfulness to our practice that we can begin to really see ourselves clearly. To see ourselves clearly is to bring transformation. When we know ourselves, we can go beyond ourselves.

Keep struggling and know that peace is still right here. Right now. They say silence heals; find out if that's true for yourself. Relax when you can't access it. It will come. It will come. Trusting in the unknown. Trusting in the process. Sometimes, this is the greatest work we can do in meditation.

"MASTERY REQUIRES ENDURANCE. MASTERY, A WORD WE DON'T USE OFTEN, IS NOT THE EQUIVALENT OF WHAT WE MIGHT CONSIDER ITS COGNATE—PERFECTIONISM—AN INHUMAN AIM MOTIVATED BY A CONCERN WITH HOW OTHERS VIEW US. MASTERY IS ALSO NOT THE SAME AS SUCCESS—AN EVENT-BASED VICTORY BASED ON A PEAK POINT, A PUNCTUATED MOMENT IN TIME. MASTERY IS NOT MERELY A COMMITMENT TO A GOAL, BUT TO A CURVED-LINE, CONSTANT PURSUIT."[XLIII]

(Dear reader, please go to the first image of the meditation gallery at the end of the book for the painting of Bhaisajyaguru: The Medicine Buddha.)

A note on the artwork: This is the Medicine Buddha as depicted by Chen Shi Zhong, my second meditation teacher who spent many years living in the mountains with an Indo-tibetan teacher. I believe this piece of work took him hundreds of hours to complete over the span of six months. He says his artistic vision manifests naturally in meditation. The Medicine Buddha is a potential being that asks us to consider that there always exists a frequency of healing in any time and space. You can recognize The Medicine Buddha in any way you wish. You can see him in any way that is logical and resonant to you. You can throw away the idea, too. If The Medicine Buddha does exist, his intention is only to exist as a field of potential healing in all circumstances. For this to really make sense, perhaps we would have to believe in spirit or soul—something that can experience healing regardless of physical constraints.

I would like to share a story related to the great quote by Sarah Lewis above:

I remember a few summers ago, someone asked me, "What kind of meditation do you teach?" Aside from the fact that Zen masters have a way of presenting meditation as something unteachable, I struggled to answer the question. Thoughts raced through my head. *Do I talk to him about mindfulness? Do I reduce meditation to stress reduction and relaxation? Do I talk to him about a more spiritual meditation or a more logical meditation?* By now it had to have been at least five seconds, which, in a mind primed for anxiety, felt like eternity. I blurted out.

"I teach self-mastery meditation." *Ahhh, my metacognition is feeling playful. Good one, Larry! What does that even mean? Self-Mastery Meditation. SMM. Almost sounds like S and M. Okay. Focus. Focus. This guy is talking to you. Hello? Knock Knock! You're on a beach called Spanish Banks, you just finished your beer league volleyball game, and this respectable middle aged man is trying to have a real conversation with you.* "Yeah, Self-mastery meditation; I teach meditation that is accessible to all belief systems. One where you yourself hold the double -sword of accountability." *Yeah. I talk like a fucking nerd. Giddy up, Gandalf.*

MEDITATION PRIMER: ANGRY AND OPPRESSIVE ENVIRONMENTS

For the past few days I have been meditating within clouds of anger. Meditating in an environment of injustice, sexism, and oppression brings me closer to the beautifully harsh realities of life. I would like to share how I was priming myself for meditation during this time.

Meditation within darkness can be insanely fruitful. What feels impossible and counter intuitive in one moment may feel completely transformed in the next when we engage in the practice of running into reality. Meditation is choosing to be choice-less in this moment. If the moment is pain, then you run into pain. Run into confusion. Run into anger. We learn to trust that running into the truth, always, is the path of paths.

This is of course, an ideal. Hold ideals in your heart and mind but trust the process. Trust this moment right here. Trust in your distrust for the moment if you have to. Trust your pain, your anger, your confusion. You have to own your darkness if you wish to be free. You must alchemize my words and make them your own through complete internalization if they are to empower you.

My words are just little packets of energy asking you to go inward and begin carving out your own method and path. Don't get too focused on what I am saying. Feel the energy and intent behind them.

It's okay if all you hear is your own mind. It's okay if you feel deafened by the silence. It's okay if you feel overwhelmed by bullshit. The way out is in. Go toward the resistance. Go toward the stress. Walk the direction (mentally or physically) that makes the butterflies in your stomach flourish and thank them for communicating with you.

I'm not saying this is easy. I'm not saying I have personally achieved peace. What I am saying is that this direction of living is fruitful. Embracing darkness. Courting confusion. Dancing in fire. Resting in uncertainty. These are the oxymoronic freedoms we can begin to taste with the practice of meditation. Don't forget, we meditate to save and realize ourselves. It is in our own awakening that we do the most for others.

"I HAVE DECIDED TO BE HAPPY, BECAUSE IT IS GOOD FOR MY HEALTH"[XLIV]

I am sick today. How I handle sickness sure has changed since I started a meditation practice. Today's meditation: I take full responsibility for the energy I bring into all situations, even if I am feeling unwell. I accept all circumstance and will work to see the light in all areas of darkness. I understand that getting sick is a signal from my body telling me to slow down. I give myself permission to be weak, vulnerable, and open. For it is friction that polishes and transforms us. I am grateful for life and understand that every single human being is subject to sickness, frailty, and death. I choose to see the interconnectivity of humanity with regard to sickness and struggle. May you all have a wonderful evening. Breathing in, I am aware I am breathing in. Breathing out, slightly stuffy, I am aware I am breathing out. Becoming conscious of the breath returns me to the present moment and reconnects my mind and body.

"WHATEVER COMES, LET IT COME, WHATEVER STAYS, LET IT STAY, WHATEVER GOES, LET IT GO"[XLV]

Many meditation teachers and scholars talk about an expansion of consciousness in meditation. Some teachers say our awareness is inherently spacious and always full of possibility, and that we just have to realize it. Others say that with practice, and diligence, we can cultivate a broader and clearer experience of consciousness. What I have experienced is that the vehicle in which I experience life does seem to expand. Awareness does deepen and broaden, and this has a variety of interesting effects.

The point I want to make, however, is that I have NEVER wanted to go back to the way I was after having any sort of mind-expanding experience. Whether it was letting a belief system crumble or something more unquantifiable like an increased feeling of spaciousness, I have never had the desire to look back. I can be overly nostalgic but with regard to meditation and the effects of meditation, I have never even felt the slightest inclination to turn my head around.

The funny thing is, an expansion of awareness on the inward path isn't always fun. As your awareness grows you find that life is not only love and light. There are many paradoxes and harshly bitter-tasting things in this existence. There is no utopia except for the one you make. Some of my experiences with meditation have been very painful. Just breathing right? Ha ha ha. But it has always been worth it. I would never ask the universe to take back the friction that affected me.

We are standing at the edge of the universe right now; this moment has never been uncovered before. I like to ask myself if everything I thought, said, and did today was exactly what I wanted to do in that moment as I prepare for bed. Let yourself unfurl freely. Pain is inevitable, suffering optional.

GIVE ME THE WHOLE PICTURE, MOTHERFUCKER

A meditator is neither a pessimist nor an optimist. From my perspective, meditation tends to take us to a place of positivity as a result of always seeing the whole picture. A meditator by nature is interested in truth. Not the just the truth that serves us, but the whole truth. The ugly truth, the unfortunate truth, and the beautiful truth. Striving to understand the whole picture may indeed be a never-ending practice; however, it is this practice that brings us to a space of awe and authentic presence, time after time.

"If you're lost and you look and you will find me, time after time."[xlvi]

Meditation is a long journey. Meditation is a lifelong journey. Meditation is the practice of familiarity.

At first when we attempt to observe ourselves without judgment, we may be overwhelmed. I certainly was. However, as the practice progressed, I saw for myself that it was true—I was completely unfamiliar with my own internal landscape.

As practice deepens and evolves, thoughts begin to take on a new life. We begin to see that thoughts have their own direction and unique birthplace within our consciousness. We see which energetic channels within stand on foundations of fear or freedom. We begin to see our own processes with immense clarity and insight. We begin to notice that there is a gap between thoughts. An undying interest in the tunnels and passages of consciousness begins to develop.

What we see clearly cannot restrict us. With a similar tone, I contend we cannot let go of what we do not fully own and understand.

Developing clarity of vision internally lends us a certain amount of trust in our own process. Synchronicities begin to shine through in the place of coincidence. Life is turbulent, but a sense of belonging begins to take over everywhere we step. Every mistake becomes a lesson, every triumph reflects on our insight and internal environment.

Blessings, my friends. May the truth of every moment reveal itself to you easily.

RUNNING INTO REALITY

A meditation scholar from the Theravaden Forest tradition once told me that meditation is running into reality. *Running into reality? What? I am already in reality. Whatever do you mean??* As the years have passed in my meditation practice, I believe what he was telling me was to insist on being myself, no matter the circumstance. When you sit down to meditate today, INSIST on being yourself. When your mind becomes agitated and rebellious, insist on being that. Let the agitation and rebellion rise up and do its thing while you observe with great ease and loving concentration. I know, great ease and great concentration are seemingly contradictory, but it can be done. Just be open to the idea that it can be done—and be gentle toward yourself if you can't today. Any energy spent toward yourself is not energy wasted. Now, back to the meditation. Run into your reality. What is your reality right now at this very second? The knot in your gut, dive into it. The darkness in your heart, gaze into it. The tightness in your throat, breathe into it. Observe all aspects of yourself with openness while maintaining an awareness of the breath. When the mind shouts *STOP! I can't do this anymore! Get up!*—give yourself a smile and go on with your day.

IDEALISM AND GAGGING

"We are awakening from the false dream we have been relentlessly sold and have relentlessly bought. It is, in fact, a nightmare paradigm of a commodified world, a lifeless world of objects, separation, and scarcity. We are awakening to a new possibility where the true abundance of this earth is no longer hoarded. Where relationships are not transactions. Where your well being is my well being is the planet's well being."[xlvii]

The more I meditate the more I can digest idealism without gagging. There is so much beauty in this world. At the same time, there is a horrendous amount of suffering. As Rumi said, yesterday I was clever, so I wanted to change the world. Today I am wise, so I changing myself. If we all commit to being true to ourselves, to being the you-est you possible, will we one day wake up in a completely new reality? Even if we can't see the future clearly, we can start where we are. Meditation is taking steps without seeing the staircase. Zen masters talk about resting in uncertainty. Does it sound just nuts to be able to do so??? Start where you are. Give thanks to your feet for being where they are. Put one ahead of the other and step into the unknown with a smile. That will be my lifelong practice. Wishing you all a wonderful day

THINK UNCONDITIONALLY

Think unconditionally eh? How meditative. I think some would agree with me if I said that meditation is the practice of thinking unconditionally. Oftentimes I hear people stressing about not grasping or overly attaching to the good experiences in life. What I don't hear, however, is the discussion of aversion to pain, darkness, and suffering. You see, with meditation, and life, it's all about balance. When you sit down to meditate you must allow yourself to think unconditionally.

You are trying to develop an affectionate concentration toward yourself no matter the circumstance. Good or bad, dark or light, heaven or hell. See it all with eyes of openness, discernment, and compassion. Keep watching. Keep observing. Keep practicing. When the mind has had its fill of thinking unconditionally without judgment, it will evolve. It will expand. It will transcend itself. That is my experience. You will develop a sense of awe toward yourself. This awe will naturally extend to those around you and the universe at large. That is my experience. Wishing you all an amazing day. Rock it!!!

TUNNEL

Meditation is like a tunnel that we can learn to peek and adventure into within ourselves. Through affectionate observation, our mental landscape becomes more familiar. Through familiarity, we all might discover such a path inward within. Watch out. You might get addicted to yourself. You might fall in love with yourself. Time and time again you will come back to yourself. You will become curious. The field of the unknown within you is vast and spacious. Perhaps even infinite.

Are you willing to peek into the rabbit hole?

WHEN SOMETHING GOES WRONG IN YOUR LIFE, JUST YELL PLOT TWIST AND MOVE THE FUCK ON.

This is meditation. Practice this at a microcosmic level. Sit down to meditate and just experience the present moment as much as possible. Truck horn blasts by? Shift attention to the breath and move on. Internal dialogue becomes insane and deafening? Shift awareness to the present moment and move on. Meditation is about surfing all the crazy waves of life. When you sit down you are going into the session with the idea that it is possible for you to find peace, joy, and equanimity in every moment. And when you can't find it, you smile to yourself. *Swerve!* Plot twist!!!

Dust yourself off and try again. Try again. Try again.

R.I.P. Aliyah. R I P. Yeap.

FORGET MORALITY. FORGET GOD. FORGET YOUR PLANS AND JUST GO.

"People are often unreasonable, irrational, and self-centered. Forgive them anyway.

If you are kind, people may accuse you of selfish, ulterior motives.

Be kind anyway.

If you are successful, you will win some unfaithful friends and some genuine enemies.

Succeed anyway.

If you are honest and sincere people may deceive you.

Be honest and sincere anyway.

What you spend years creating, others could destroy overnight.

Create anyway.

If you find serenity and happiness, some may be jealous.

Be happy anyway.

The good you do today, will often be forgotten.

Do good anyway.

Give the best you have, and it will never be enough.

Give your best anyway.

In the final analysis, it is between you and God.

It was never between you and them anyway."[xlviii]

When asked about a creator God, the Buddha remained silent.

The mystics all over the world say God is within you.

Christ said the seed of his consciousness is in each and every one of us. He loved lepers and whores without condition.

The Egyptians say the kingdom of heaven is revealed to those who know themselves.

You will find various Hindu traditions that say Brahman (God) is within you and you are within Brahman.

Although these lines of thought resonate with me, I suggest we put them aside. Forget about being good. Forget about being moral. Forget about enlightenment, heaven, and saintliness. Just know that everything you do, you do to yourself.

Despite our interdependent nature, we come into this alone and we leave this world alone. Even with a lover tangled around us, we fall asleep alone inside our consciousness. Everything you do, you live and die with. Be mindfully, truthfully selfish.

"All know the path, few walk it."[xlix]

CRYBABY

It was the summer before I was diagnosed with lung cancer. At this point I had done about 1000 hours of meditation. I was in Taiwan, in Yi-Lan, a half-urbanized country province on the northeastern coast of the island. Formosa, the Portuguese called it. I was residing quite contently on the rooftop of our animal medicine factory where my Grandmother and Grandfather kept a vibrant array of subtropical plants and shrubberies. It was an awesome hangout, even if it was overly humid and prone to mosquito swarm invasions. It must have been around 7pm. I was sitting in meditation on the stony floor. Barefoot and dirty. The way I like it. It felt like it had been maybe twenty minutes of practice. I opened my eyes quickly, I remember. The clouds were a solid grey with light blue overtones. The air had a complex sensation as I closed my eyes again. *Might as well keep sitting here*, I thought; I was in a quiet little country cranny where there is little night life. I continued to sit with a mix of mindfulness and concentration practice. I started to feel a sense of deepness not so common in my everyday practice.

I feel like my consciousness is like a stone. I am sinking. I am falling. I am being pulled into something. I feel a surge of energy inside throwing itself up into my eyes. I am tearing up. I am beginning to sob. I want to open my eyes but I can't. I feel like I am tapping into the sorrows of the universe. All the injustice, rapes, seemingly meaningless deaths. I hate you Buddha. I hate you Universe. I see visions of skulls, deaths, tortures in my mind's eye. It's like there is an eye I can't turn off inside me. All I can feel is immense pain, sadness, repression, and claustrophobia. I feel like I am in an MRI of suffering.

I am violently sobbing and weeping on the floor in a garden on the roof of a Taiwanese chemical factory.

A VISUAL DISPLAY OF MEDITATION WITH WORDS

JUST SIT DOWN

Without practice, meditation and mindfulness are just words. Without practice, heart-centered insights never develop and all you have are knowledge and head games. Knowledge and intelligence are outward games; wisdom is an inward process.

SIT DOWN.

I cannot teach you anything. I can inspire you, confuse you, contort you, and perhaps even guide you. However, there is nothing I can say to convince the deepest questionings of your soul. This door, this path. You open, you walk.

SIT DOWN

I keep repeating myself because the idea that you are your own greatest teacher is a difficult pill to swallow. Do these words just float past your consciousness?

SIT DOWN

It is when you are resistant that the practice is most powerful.

SIT DOWN

The universe is self-organizing. Nature is self-organizing. Get out of your own way. Let your life force self-organize. Develop trust and familiarity with yourself. Commit to falling and getting up.

SIT DOWN

Don't believe everything you think.

SIT DOWN

Entertain your mind but be not its servant. Entertain emotions but be not their play toy.

SIT DOWN

A minute of practice is worth more than ninety minutes of mental meandering.

SIT DOWN

What good are your ideals if you don't trust the process? Look for the seeds of your ideals within the process.

SIT DOWN

Mindfulness is just a word if you don't root into this moment. The mind can rationalize ANYTHING. Be here. Now!

SIT DOWN

Just sit. Let the mind go crazy. This is the process. See the futile hamster wheel that is self-judgment. See the inherent lack of guarantee in your endless planning. See the immature glorification of busy and begin to tune into the divine process that is you.

SIT DOWN

Forget relaxation. You can buy relaxation. You can't buy meditation. You are sitting. Priming. Processing. Realizing. Transforming.

SIT DOWN

You're bored? Then you are bored with yourself. This is the territory of potential awakening and genius. Don't let petty boredom get in your way.

SIT DOWN

Only when your roots stretch fully into the darkness can you truly shine.

SIT DOWN

Open up. Open in. Harness. Witness. Practice.

PRACTICE

PRACTICE

PRACTICE

Ever tried, ever failed, no matter. Try again, fail again, fail better.

HERE ARE SOME BONUS MEDITATION RELATED PASSAGES I WROTE AFTER THE MANUSCRIPT WAS FINISHED AND EDITED.

1

Meditation makes it easier to generate motivation. As awareness itself deepens, expands, and transforms through meditation practices that evolve consciousness, the mind cannot help but find the generation of focus, creativity, and motivation naturally.

It doesn't always feel good but that doesn't mean the practice isn't worthwhile. Befriend all aspects of yourself. Pay attention to all teachings but respect the master within and honour the intuition, even if you make a "mistake".

2

Part of the meditative path is slowly becoming intensely aware of where exactly each thought, emotion, and mental phenomena manifest from. Meditation should lead you to a place where self empowerment is completely natural. By becoming highly aware of your internal processes, you will be able to understand, embrace, and thus transcend fear. Fear is not an enemy, fear is a messenger. The question is how will you use the information within fear to enable you to make choices based on your deepest loves and hopes.

As you continually and consistently meditate, you will find that any practice that directs your conscious energy inward begins to grant you a type of knowledge of the self that seems both utterly obvious yet incredulous at the same time. To find the magic in the mundane will change your life!

As you quiet the mind and you find yourself quiet in your mind you may discover you are not quite your mind. You are something much much more!!

3

There is something about Meditation that keeps me coming back with more passion day after day. By consistently training, examining, and challenging the mind in a lively and personal way, I can find that there is much more to meditation than just finding calm and relaxation.

I have found that there is such a depth of treasure and magic inside human consciousness that I cannot help but continually harass you all on Instagram about it. Quite honestly, the internal voice within always saw myself as a big piece of shit so I see no reason why any other human being can't find the magic-ness within meditation and knowledge of the self.

There is something more to meditation after we have found the ability to be more equanimous and sincerely present in all circumstances. Aside from continually embracing human impulses in a mindful and playful way, meditation can show us that the universe within is infinite and expansive, in accordance with the outer physical universe. There is a depth of knowledge and experience within human consciousness that is accessible to us all and it seems to me, after careful study, that this type of knowledge can be helpful and inspiring to all different kinds of human beings and personalities.

We can all discover the gap between thoughts and begin to learn how to navigate the automated aspects of mind. We can all discover that our human awareness can be radically transformed through internal practices. We can all find the mystical experience inside that is yearning to be harmonized with the modern world. We can all find that light or spark inside that makes ideas such as "Namasté" incredibly visceral and true.

Don't make it a separation between mind body and spirit. Look inside and find the inseparability of such concepts and begin to see interconnectivity from perspectives previously unknown.

Continually shine the light of your awareness onto itself. Give yourself love, attention, and non-judgment. Dig at yourself continually and find gems within. Meditate to find expansion and radical transformation.

4

Om Mani Padme Hum.

Pronounced like Aum Ma Nay Pay May Hum.

Om Mani Padme Hum.

Tibetan ideals in concentrated form. This mantra represents a Buddhist figure often symbolized as an emanation of great compassion. The mantra is associated with the attainment of wisdom, empathy, and the ability to resonate deeply with others. It was initially presented to me as a tool to build concentration of mind. I do believe one can benefit from mantra chanting even without belief and faith. A great doubting is more than acceptable in many schools of meditative thought. Skepticism and flexibility.

Om Mani Padme Hum.

Om Mani Padme Hum.

Om Mani Padme Hum.

A mantra is a phrase that the mind adorns. You chant it as often as you can out-loud or quietly to yourself as a way to increase the weight of your mind. A warrior may purposely wear heavy gear to increase the intensity of his training, a meditator carries internally a mantra as a way of continually training the non physical aspects of life and consciousness.

Om Mani Padme Hum.

Om Mani Padme Hum.

See it as sacred, see it as silly. I humbly contend that it does not matter how one chooses to identify with the idea of mantra. What is important is you put in the reps.

Perhaps you strictly see it as a mental tool. Perhaps you believe these are sacred vowels that connect us somehow to higher powers. Perhaps you believe chanting the names of deities creates a certain response that you can feel. Perhaps, like me, you believe that the human being is an antenna and certain practices can shape the way we connect with the universe at large.

Om Mani Padme Hum.

Om Mani Padme Hum.

Om Mani Padme Hum.

Every time you complain, think of this phrase. Use it as a marker for negative thoughts by the brain. By studying the thoughts and in increasing the amount of attention we shine inward, we inspire changes in behavior and emotion simply by being more aware of our own programming and negativity. A mantra can trigger us to continually challenge our own assumptions and beliefs.

Om Mani Padme Hum.

Om Mani Padme Hum.

Om Mani Padme Hum.

5

With meditation, you start to see that you are more than what the mind plans and calculates you to be. You are the one who is aware of mind, not mind itself. By facing all states of the mind with compassion and openness, we learn enough about the mind to know we are beyond it. By losing ourselves on one level, we find unlimited strength to really be ourselves on another. Meditation is a pathway to this experience and

I contend that it is an experience that can radically improve your life.

6

I know guys. I know gals. Shit is fucked up. World is corrupt. Pain is everywhere. Injustice all over. Repression of expression and stiflings of the soul are all too common. Our modern age worships the clever ego and dismisses the intelligence of the heart.

I know your life might be absolute shit right now. I feel your pain in my meditations. However, we can build a sanctuary in our minds. The grass is green where you water it. Start with the mind. Start with the breathe. Do what you can with what you have, wherever you are.

Wishing you all a wonderful everything.

Lokah Samasatah Sukhino Bhavantu.

7

Meditation is not just about mindfulness, peace, and relaxation. It is about uncovering your authentic self, the one you have buried under other people's needs and projections. Meditation is about your own journey. No one can be the master of your path except for you.

MEDITATIVE IMAGE GALLERY BY MASTER CHEN SHI ZHONG OF LUODONG-TAIWAN.

The following images are all hand painted by my second meditation teacher Chen Shi Zhong. Master Chen is an artist, teacher, medicine man, and all around meditation practitioner, studying all schools of thought related to meditation. He does a meditation practice before and after all his painting sessions and his paintings are embedded with his wisdom and good intentions for everyone. These pictures may be used as objects for concentration meditation and you are encouraged to develop your own meaning and frame of reference around them.

Although the artwork is mostly Buddhist, the wisdom and healing contained within the images are open to all.

Everyone can heal

Everyone can know

Om Mani Padme Hum

Everyone can do

Gaze Raptly

Your fury has knowledge, listen in the heat

The colors within

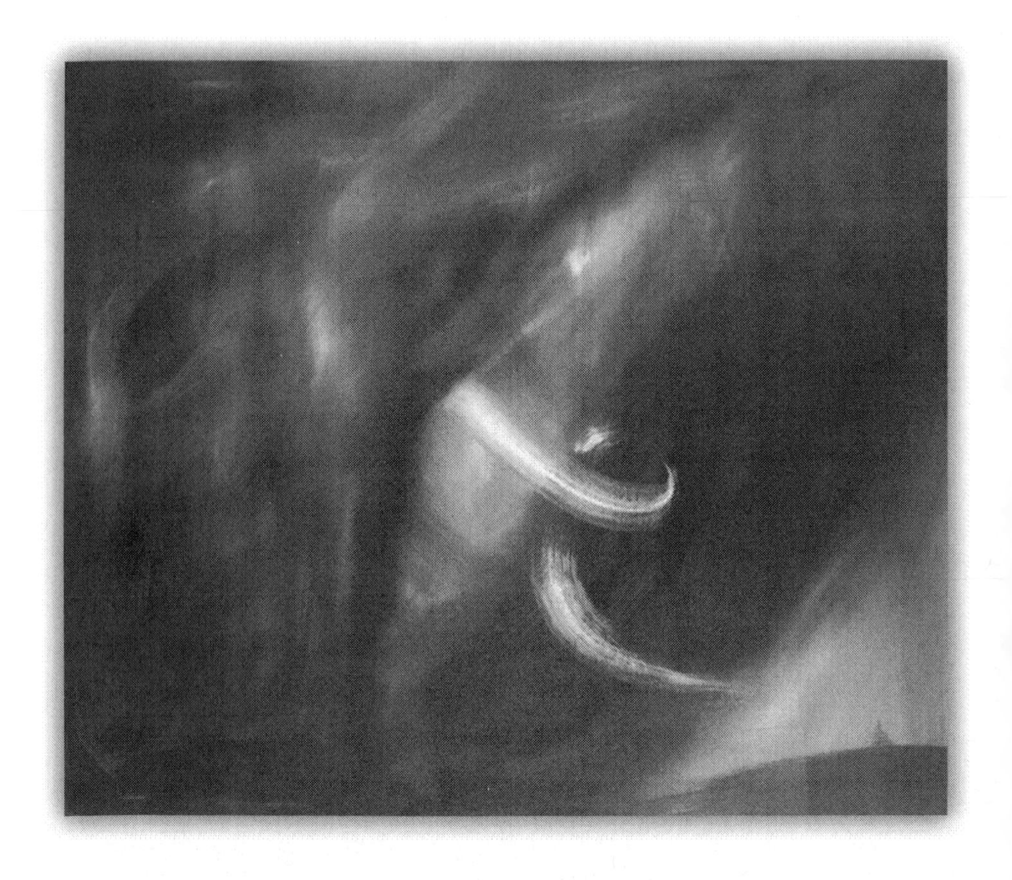

Everyone deserves compassion

Connect with the Universe

QUOTES

[i] "If you want to build a ship, don't drum up people to collect wood and don't assign them tasks and work, but rather teach them to long for the endless immensity of the sea." ~ Antoine de Saint Exupéry

[ii] "Open at your own speed, but open. Dig what's happening to you. By 'dig' I mean get into it. There are lessons for you there. And when it gets uncomfortable, that's an important time to open and dig." ~ Jeff Bridges

[iii] "I don't like to be out of my comfort zone, which is about a half an inch wide." ~ Larry David

[iv] "Bite, Chew, Suck." ~ "March of the Pigs," by Trent Reznor, Nine Inch Nails

[v] "I wonder how much of what weighs me down is not mine to carry." ~ Aditi (net blogger)

[vi] "Sometimes I can feel my bones straining under the weight of all the lives I'm not living." ~ Jonathan Safran Foer

[vii] "Ever tried, ever failed, no matter. Try again. Fail again. Fail better."~ Sam Beckett

[viii] "The rules you were given were the rules that worked for the person who created them. When you're mindful, rules, routines, and goals guide you; they don't govern you." ~ Ellen Langer

[ix] "Learn the rules like a pro, so you can break them like an artist." ~ Pablo Picasso

[x.] "Following all the rules leaves a completed checklist. Following your heart achieves a completed you." ~ Ray Davis

[xi.] "You gotta be bold, you gotta be bad, you gotta be wiser. You gotta be hard, you gotta be tough, you gotta be stronger." ~ Des'ree and Ashley Ingram

[xii.] "I am the master of my fate, I am the captain of my soul." ~ William Henry, *Invictus*

[xiii.] "He asked, 'What makes a man a writer?' 'Well,' I said, 'it's simple. You either get it down on paper, or jump off a bridge.'" ~ Charles Bukowski

[xiv.] "If you think you are enlightened, go spend a week with your family." ~ Ram Dass (Richard Alpert)

[xv.] "Unwholesome action, hurting self, comes easily. Wholesome action, healing self, takes effort." ~ Thícht Nhãt Hanh

[xvi.] "Yoga is like music: the rhythm of the body, the melody of the mind, and the harmony of the soul create the symphony of life." ~ BKS Iyengar

[xvii.] "I don't wait, I marinate." ~ Rapper Big Sean.

[xviii.] "Give love and then forget you gave it." ~ Larry Li (surprise!)

[xix.] "Act without expectation." ~ Lao Tzu

[xx.] "Wisdom is knowing I am nothing, Love is knowing I am everything, and between the two my life moves." ~ Nisargadatta Maharaj.

xxi. "If you truly loved yourself, you could never hurt another." ~ Unknown (although often falsely attributed to Buddha)

xxii. "I contend that this world does not need more monks in caves; this world needs more wizards in the city." ~ Larry Li

xxiii. "Tradition is the illusion of permanence." ~ Woody Allen

xxiv. "The world is full of magic things, patiently waiting for our senses to grow sharper." ~ W.B. Yeats

xxv. "And those who were seen dancing were thought to be insane by those who could not hear the music." ~ Nietzsche

xxvi. "If the doors of perception were cleansed everything would appear to man as it is, infinite." ~ William Blake

xxvii. "You cannot rip the skin off the snake. The snake must moult the skin." ~ Ram Dass (Richard Alpert)

xxviii. "To be yourself in a world that is constantly trying to make you something else is the greatest accomplishment." ~ Ralph Waldo Emerson

xxix. "You are standing on a bridge watching yourself go by." ~ Ram Dass (Richard Alpert)

xxx. "Ever tried. Ever failed. No matter. Try again. Fail again. FAIL BETTER." ~ Samuel Beckett

xxxi. "Wisdom is knowing I am nothing, Love is knowing I am everything, and in between the two my life moves." ~ Sri Nisargadatta Maharaj [xxxii] "All I can do is be me, whoever that is." ~ Bob Dylan

[xxxiii] "The Japanese say you have three faces. The first face, you show to the world. The second face, you show to your close friends, and your family. The third face, you never show anyone. It is the truest reflection of who you are." ~ Unknown

[xxxiv] "Man cannot remake himself without suffering, for he is both marble and sculptor." ~ Alexis Carrel

[xxxv] "I have no special talent, I am only passionately curious." ~ Albert Einstein

[xxxvi] "Righteousness is a golden chain." ~ often attributed to Ram Dass (Richard Alpert)

[xxxvii] "My religion is not deceiving myself." ~ Milarepa

[xxxviii] "I would rather be slapped by the truth than kissed with a lie." ~ Russian proverb

[xxxix] "Be humble for you are made of earth. Be noble for you are made of stars." ~ Serbian Proverb

[xl] "Just watch how our world is changing how people are changing. You contribute each time you show your mastery over your own choices for the essence of your Being rather than your reaction to the illusion." ~ Unknown Kundalini practitioner

[xli] "I myself am made entirely of flaws, stitched together with good intentions." ~ Augusten Burroughs

xlii. "Meditation is running into reality." ~ Master Bhante

xliii. "Mastery requires endurance. Mastery, a word we don't use often, is not the equivalent of what we might consider its cognate—perfectionism—an inhuman aim motivated by a concern with how others view us. Mastery is also not the same as success—an event-based victory based on a peak point, a punctuated moment in time. Mastery is not merely a commitment to a goal, but to a curved-line, constant pursuit." ~ Sarah Lewis

xliv. "I have decided to be happy, because it is good for my health." ~ Voltaire

xlv. "Whatever comes, let it come, whatever stays, let it stay, whatever goes, let it go." ~ Unknown as to exactly who has said this, but it is a very prominent Zen idea/line of thought; the trick is to lose expectations while being more open to possible disappointment, so this idea is preached.

xlvi. "If you're lost and you look and you will find me, time after time." ~ Cyndi Lauper and Rob Hyman

xlvii. "We are awakening from the false dream we have been relentlessly sold and have relentlessly bought. It is, in fact, a nightmare paradigm of a commodified world, a lifeless world of objects, separation, and scarcity. We are awakening to a new possibility where the true abundance of this earth is no longer hoarded. Where relationships are not transactions. Where your well being is my well being is the planet's well being." ~ Velcrow Ripper

xlviii. "People are often unreasonable, irrational, and self-centered. Forgive them anyway.

If you are kind, people may accuse you of selfish, ulterior motives.

Be kind anyway.

If you are successful, you will win some unfaithful friends and some genuine enemies.

Succeed anyway.

If you are honest and sincere people may deceive you.

Be honest and sincere anyway.

What you spend years creating, others could destroy overnight.

Create anyway.

If you find serenity and happiness, some may be jealous.

Be happy anyway.

The good you do today, will often be forgotten.

Do good anyway.

Give the best you have, and it will never be enough.

Give your best anyway.

In the final analysis, it is between you and God.

It was never between you and them anyway."

~ (An adaptation of Kent M. Keith's Paradoxical Commandments, often attributed to Mother Theresa)

xlix. "All know the path, few walk it." ~ Bodhidharma

ABOUT THE AUTHOR

Larry Li holds a BA in philosophy and honors in holistic nutrition, and he is in the process of studying Ayurveda and special intervention for autism. He works one-on-one with clients as a healer, counselor, and meditation facilitator. Having previously specialized in OCD-related disorders, he is now branching out and is interested in developing meditation techniques for youth, especially those with special needs.

Larry has battled apathy, anxiety, and depression and been diagnosed with Graves's disease and lung cancer. As someone who used to be overweight, hates authority, can't sit still, and is generally hedonistic, he considers his journey to becoming a meditation proponent an interesting ride, and now, he's sharing his story to inspire others.

This book is also a means to pay it forward. It contains the teachings given to Larry by teachers all around the globe.

Made in the USA
Charleston, SC
28 May 2016